Foreign Corrupt Practices Act:

Fundamentals and Practices

By Marcus Goncalves

ASME PRESS

Library of Congress Cataloging-in-Publication Data

Names: Goncalves, Marcus.
Title: The Foreign Corrupt Practice Act : fundamentals and practices / by Marcus Goncalves.
Other titles: Foreign Corrupt Practices Act
Description: New York : ASME Press, 2016. | Includes bibliographical
    references and index.
Identifiers: LCCN 2016016142 | ISBN 978-0-7918-6123-3
Subjects: LCSH: United States. Foreign Corrupt Practices Act of 1977 |
    Corporations, American--Law and legislation--United States--Criminal   provisions. |
Bribery--Law and legislation--United States.
Classification: LCC KF9351.A3281977 G66 2016 | DDC 345.73/02323--dc23 LC record
available at https://lccn.loc.gov/2016016142

Table of Contents

Acknowledgement

I would like to thank, yet again, Mary Grace Stefanchik, the editor at the American Society of Mechanical Engineers (ASME), not only for publishing yet another one of my works for ASME's collection, but especially for her continuous patience during the production phase of this book.

Dedication

To my wife Carla, sons Samir and Josh (in memory), and my princess Andrea (also in memory), the true joy of my life. To God be the glory!

Marcus Goncalves,
Spring 2016

Chapter 1 – The Challenge of Global Corruption

Overview

For the last twenty years or so, we have witnessed rapid development in the effort to combat corruption under international law. Corruption is one of the world's most pervasive problems, affecting international trade, environmental protection efforts, human rights, national security, access to health care and justice services, economic development, and the legitimacy of governments around the world. Efforts to prevent or reduce corrupt practices have been just as diverse, and have met with varying degrees of success.

Legal and policy solutions to the challenge of corruption have proliferated, but relatively recent legal developments such as the United Nations Convention Against Corruption have yet to be tested in practice. In addition, a significant gap continues to exist between laws on paper and implementation of anti-corruption policies in practice.

We now live in a world where, according to Transparency International,[1] and as illustrated in Figure 1.1, more than one in four people report having paid a bribe. International criminals and dishonest businessmen don't hesitate to make use of loose regulatory systems put in place by politicians in certain "safe haven" countries around the world to attract capital.

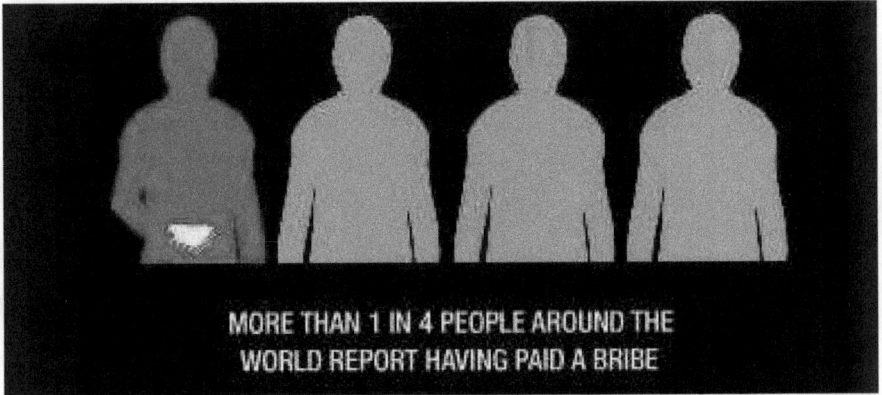

MORE THAN 1 IN 4 PEOPLE AROUND THE
WORLD REPORT HAVING PAID A BRIBE

Figure 1.1 – More than one in four people around the world report having paid a bribe. SOURCE: Transparency International

Currently there are two regional anti-corruption conventions that are in force. The first convention was negotiated and adopted by the members of the Organization of American States (OAS),[2] while the second was adopted under the auspices of the Organization for Economic Co-operation and Development (OECD).[3] In addition, a number of international organizations are consistently devoting

[1] Transparency International Secretariat (2013) Media Advisory: Major Exporters still lag in enforcing rules against foreign bribery, Transparency International, 10/02/2013, http://www.transparency.org/news/pressrelease/bribe_paying_still_very_high_worldwide_but _people_ready_to_fight_back, last accessed on 12/14/2013.

[2] Organization of American States: Inter-American Convention Against Corruption, Mar. 29, 1996, 35 I.L.M. 724.

[3] Convention on Combating Bribery of Foreign Public Officials in International Business Transactions, Done at Paris, Dec. 18, 1997, 37 I.L.M. The OECD Convention was signed on November 21, 1997 by the twenty-six member countries of the Organization of Economic Co-operation and Development and by five nonmember countries: Argentina, Brazil, Bulgaria, Chile and the Slovak Republic.

resources to this subject. These groups include several bodies within the UN, the EU, and the International Bank for Reconstruction and Development (IBRD), also known as the World Bank Group (WB). Also involved are several non-governmental organizations, such as Transparency International and the International Chamber of Commerce (ICC).

Figure 1.2 provides the perceived corruption levels by country and companies' propensity to bribe. The highest the score the fewer propensities a country have to offer bribes.

Perceived corruption levels by country and companies' propensity to bribe

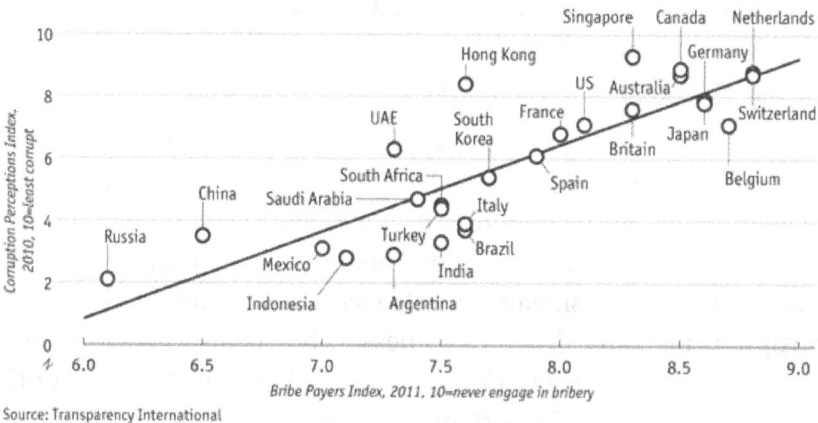

Source: Transparency International

Figure 1.2 - The perceived corruption levels by country and companies' propensity to bribe. SOURCE: Transparency International.

When journalists with the Center for Investigative Journalism in Bucharest, Romania started investigating a gold mining operation in the village of Rosia Montana, in the heart of Transylvania, they didn't know they would soon be looking at a far wider web of corruption that linked commercial enterprises on five continents. The name of a company and the name of its founder led the journalists to Russian oligarchs, officials in Eastern European governments, former employees of well-known corporations and even North Atlantic Treaty Organization (NATO)[4] officials.

The tangled network of connections unraveled as journalists looked deeper and deeper at corporate records in more than 20 countries. Company records exposed the connections between former Communist government officials and devious, Western-based companies, as well as the fact that big chunks of Eastern European economies are still handled by former employees of the Communist secret services.

In another example, a name in a corporate record in Bulgaria led to an investigation into the Irish Republican Army's (IRA) money laundering through purchases of real estate on the shores of the Black Sea. A company record in Hungary led to one of the most powerful Russian organized crime bosses and his questionable interests in the natural gas industry.

When we consider these examples, and there are plenty of news outlets around the world showcasing many more, we must also consider ways of responding to the challenges of dealing with international corruption and crime, not only as international business investors and professionals, but also as a responsible global society. Corruption not only disrupt businesses, but is also generates social imbalances and poverty. The international response to corruption, therefore, raises many important questions:

- Could global corruption and crime be a manifestation of oppression around the world, part of a global outcry against the abuse of power?
- Is the pressure on trade competition around the globe promoting corruption?

---

[4] NATO is an international organization composed of the US, Canada, UK, and a number of European countries, established by the North Atlantic Treaty (1949) for purposes of collective security.

- Is global corruption a result of globalization, or the consequence of a renewed sense of morality around the world?
- Should global corruption be a concern for international law?

While certainly provoked by these questions, this chapter does not pretend to give definite answers to these questions. It seeks only to contribute to the understanding of the development of anti-corruption measures under international law, since, according to the United Nations Interregional Crime and Justice Research Institute (UNICRI), corruption today is one of the main threats to global development and security.[5] It also sets the stage in which the U.S. Foreign Corrupt Practices Act (FCPA) was developed in 1977. Corruption and crime is often considered the negative side of globalization as international crime has been rapidly capitalizing on the expansion of global trade and broadening its range of activity. Several criminal groups, organized as multinational companies, are often seeking profits through the evaluation of countries' risks, benefits and markets analysis.

Combating Corruption Around the World

For entities fighting crime and corruption around the world, one of the main challenges, therefore, consists in preventing such groups from continuously adapting to the changes at local and international levels. It is important to disrupt the creation of intercontinental networks, and prevent them from diversifying their activities and taking advantage of the potential offered by globalization. These factors are the main obstacles for all the entities around the world fighting organized crime. Furthermore, the lack of judicial and enforcement tools plays a strategic role in the growth of global criminal syndicates' management of trafficking drugs, arms, human beings, counterfeiting and money laundering.

---

[5] http://www.unicri.it/topics/organized_crime_corruption/

Under the veil of banking and commercial secrecy laws, huge amounts of money exchange hands in such havens outside the jurisdiction scrutiny of the source countries. Capital cycled through such dealings can be transformed into real estate, bonds or other goods and then moved back into the country or to other global markets legitimately. Such transactions are closely looked at by international law enforcement because they raise suspicions of money laundering associated with organized crime and terrorism.

Although offshore havens are usually associated with tropical islands somewhere in the Caribbean, in many instances countries such as Austria, Switzerland, or the U.S. have offshore-like facilities that enable businesses and individuals to hide ownership and deter investigators from finding out who owns companies that are involved in crooked deals.

Organized crime figures would rather use *private foundations* (Privatstiftungs) in Austria, or companies in the state of Delaware in the U.S., than companies in the British Virgin Islands (BVI), the Isle of Man, Aruba or Liberia, known as safe havens that the media and law enforcement has associated as a place for money laundering and shady deals. This is because the mere mentioning of any of these places can put a red flag on a transaction that is then monitored by international law enforcement.

All over the world, organized crime adopts all forms of corruption to infiltrate political, economic and social levels. Although strong institutions, in particular government ones, are supposed to be impermeable to corruption, weak governance often coexists with corruption and a mutually causal connection exists between corruption and feeble governmental institutions, which often ends up in a vicious cycle. Hence, well-known offshore havens are fighting to clean up their names and show that proper control mechanisms are in place. It should be mentioned that in most cases, such jurisdictions now are used for tax purposes.

For instance, Liechtenstein, a European country of 35,000 people located in the Alps, was hit hard in the beginning of 2008 when data stolen by a former bank employee were sold to law enforcement agencies in many European countries. The data showed that wealthy citizens from many countries have used Liechtenstein's banks in tax evasion schemes.

As a result of the leak, the German authorities that bought the disks containing the information managed to recover over US$150 million U.S. dollars in back taxes within months of obtaining the data. The U.S., Canada, Australia and the EU countries are also in possession of the data and are pursuing their own investigations into tax evasion involving banking in the tiny country.

The scandal not only shook Liechtenstein's political relationships with other countries but spread to Switzerland and Luxembourg, two other European countries that have a record of bank secrecy and non-transparent financial transactions. The head of the Swiss Bankers' Association, Pierre Mirabaud, was so outraged by the fact that the stolen data ended up in German law enforcement's hands that he said in an interview with a Swiss TV station that the methods of the German investigators reminded him of Gestapo practices, referring to the secret police of Nazi-era Germany. He later apologized for the unfortunate comparison. Just like Liechtenstein, Cyprus has been blamed many times for harboring money from organized crime groups and former communist officials from Eastern European countries.

The growing problem of offshore havens, corruption and crime, and the damage they bring to the global economy, has been pointed out again and again, in the context of the global financial crisis. The Organization for Economic Co-operation and Development (OECD) together with French and German government leaders vowed to make the offshore industry *disappear*. They called the offshore areas the *black holes of global finance*[6]. The offshore company formation industry, however, is kept alive by scores of

---

[6] Radu, Paul C. (2008) The Investigative Journalist Handbook, 12/03/2008, International Center for Journalist, https://reportingproject.net/occrp/index.php/en/cc-resource-center/handbook/191-the-investigative-journalist-handbook. Last accessed on 09/08/2012.

lawyers, incorporation agents and solicitors. They advertise complex business schemes to maximize returns and minimize taxation.

Take for example the website http://www.off-shore.co.uk/faq/company-formation/ which explicitly presents potential customers with the possibility of hiding the real ownership of a company behind a nominee shareholder or director. According to the site's frequently asked questions (FAQ) section,

> "A nominee shareholder or director is a third party who allows his/her name to be used in place of the real or beneficial owner and director of the company. The nominee is advised particularly in those jurisdictions where the names of the officers are part of a public record, open for anyone who cares to look can find out these identities. The name of the nominee will appear and ensure the privacy of the beneficial owner."

The primary role of such company formation schemes is to avoid paying taxes. However, some countries go to extremes when they try to hide the real beneficial owners. Panama and Liberia are among the countries that go to great lengths to preserve the anonymity of company owners. Under Panamanian law, an *S.A. corporation*[7] can be owned by the physical holder of certificates or shares, with no recorded owner in any database or public registry. In fact, there is no public registry in Panama, so the government does not even know who owns shares in corporations. Shares can exchange hands at any time and the beneficial owners are impossible to track down through public records.

Determining the ownership of companies trading around the world has become increasingly complex. A company in Belgrade, Serbia, could be owned by a firm in Rotterdam, the Netherlands,

---

[7] Designates a type of corporation in countries that mostly employ civil law. Depending on language, it means anonymous society, anonymous company, anonymous partnership, or Share Company, roughly equivalent to public limited company in common law jurisdictions.

which could in turn be owned by a private foundation in Austria that has Russian oligarchs as its beneficial owners. This is a common scheme. Investigative journalists in the Balkans have identified schemes as complicated as twenty layers of companies. Searches performed for names of such companies often lead to lawyers or designated shareholders. But this should not be seen as a dead end. Organized crime figures quite often rely on the same lawyers or the same formation agent when they establish new companies to limit the number of people who are aware of their moves. Once a lawyer or straw party in such a company is identified, searches on the lawyer's name can be performed on various databases. This could reveal dozens or hundreds of companies associated with the solicitor's name.

Therefore, as mentioned earlier in this chapter, corruption is a challenge not only for emerging and frontier markets but also for advanced economies. In the U.S., as a result of the U.S. Securities and Exchange Commission (SEC) investigations in the mid-1970s, over 400 U.S. companies admitted making questionable or illegal payments in excess of $300 million dollars to foreign government officials, politicians, and political parties. The abuses ran the gamut from bribery of high foreign officials to secure some type of favorable action by a foreign government to so-called facilitating payments that were made to ensure that government functionaries discharged certain ministerial or clerical duties.

Corruption Generates Poverty

Being poor does not only mean falling below a certain income line. Poverty is a multi-dimensional phenomenon that is often characterized by a series of different factors, including access to essential services (health, education, sanitation, etc.), basic civil rights, empowerment and human development.[8] Corruption undermines these development pillars, an individual's human rights

---

[8] Amartya Sen (1999) Development as Freedom, Oxford, United Kingdom: Oxford University Press, 1999.

and the legal frameworks intended to protect them. In countries where governments can pass policies and budgets without consultation or accountability for their actions, undue influence, unequal development and poverty result.[9] People become disempowered (politically, economically and socially) and, in the process, further impoverished.

In a corrupt environment, wealth is captured, income inequality is increased and a state's governing capacity is reduced, particularly when it comes to attending to the needs of the poor. For citizens, these outcomes create a scenario that leaves the poor trapped and development stalled, often forcing the poor to rely on bribes and other illegal payments in order to access basic services. For a country, the results produce multiple and destructive forces: increased corruption, reduced sustainable growth and slower rates of poverty reduction[10]. As warned by the World Bank, corruption is "the greatest obstacle to reducing poverty."[11] This growing socio-economic inequality causes the loss of confidence in public institutions. Social instability and violence increase because of the growing inequality, poverty and mass mistrust of political leaders and institutions.

In fact, when it comes to income inequality, even Alan Greenspan is worried about this troubling trend. As argued by Chrystia Freeland, a Canadian international finance reporter at

---

[9] Moore, M. (2005) Signposts to More Effective States: Responding to Governance Challenges in Developing Countries, Institute of Developing Studies, The Centre for the Future State, UK, http://www2.ids.ac.uk/gdr/cfs/pdfs/SignpoststoMoreEffectiveStates.pdf, last accessed on 12/10/2013.

[10] For more information on this theme, see Paolo Mauro, "Corruption and Growth," Quarterly Journal of Economics, 110, 681-712 (1995); Sanjeev Gupta, Hamid Davoodi and Rosa Alonso Terme, "Does Corruption Affect Income Equality and Poverty?" IMF Working Paper 98/76 (Washington, DC: IMF, 1998); Paolo Mauro, "The Effects of Corruption on Growth and Public Expenditure," Chapter 20 in Arnold J. Heidenheimer and Michael Johnston (eds.), Political Corruption: Concepts and Contexts. 3rd ed. (New Brunswick, NJ: Transaction Publishers, 2002).

[11] www.worldbank.org/anticorruption. Last accessed on 10/10/2012.

Thompson Reuters, in her book *Plutocrats,*[12] there has always been some gap between rich and poor and every country around the globe, but recently what it means to be rich has changed dramatically. Forget the 1 percent—Plutocrats proves that it is the wealthiest 0.1 percent who is outpacing the rest of us at breakneck speed. Most of these new fortunes are not inherited, amassed instead by perceptive businesspeople that see themselves as deserving victors in a cutthroat international competition. In her book, Freeland exposes the consequences of concentrating the world's wealth into fewer and fewer hands.

The question Freeland raises is whether the gap between the superrich and everybody else is the product of impersonal market forces or political machinations. She draws parallels between current inequality and the Gilded Age of the late 1800s, when the top 1 percent of the U.S. population held one-third of the national income. Globalization and the technology revolution are the major factors behind what she sees as new and overlapping gilded ages: the second for the U.S., the first for emerging markets. Drawing on interviews with economists and the elite themselves, Freeland chronicles hand wringing over the direction of the global economy by these 0.1% plutocrats around the world. As she laments, the feedback loop between money, politics, and ideas is both cause and consequence of the rise of the super-elite.

Corruption, therefore, often accompanies centralization of power, when leaders are not accountable to those they serve. More directly, corruption inhibits development when leaders help themselves to money that would otherwise be used for development projects. Corruption, both in government and business, places heavy cost on society. Businesses should enact, publicize and follow codes of conduct banning corruption on the part of their staff and directors. Citizens must demand greater transparency on the part of both government and the corporate sector and create reform movements where needed.

[12] Freeland, Chrystia, (2012) Plutocrats: the rise of the new global super-rich and the fall of everyone else, Penguin Press, New York City, NY.

Corruption on the part of governments, the private sector and citizens affects development initiatives at their very root by skewing decision-making, budgeting and implementation processes. When these actors abuse their entrusted power for private gain, corruption denies the participation of citizens and diverts public resources into private hands. The poor find themselves at the losing end of this corruption chain — without state support and the services they demand. The issue of corruption is also very much inter-related with other issues. At a global level, the economic system that has shaped the current form of globalization in the past decades requires further scrutiny for it has also created conditions whereby corruption can flourish and exacerbate the conditions of people around the world who already have little say about their own destiny.

Corruption is both a major cause and a result of poverty around the world. It occurs at all levels of society, from local and national governments, civil society, judiciary functions, large and small businesses, military and other services and so on. Corruption, nonetheless, affects the poorest the most, whether in rich or poor nations.

It is difficult to measure or compare, however, the impact of corruption on poverty against the effects of inequalities that are structured into law, such as unequal trade agreements, structural adjustment policies, "free" trade agreements and so on. The reality is that corruption and crime generates a lot of poverty around the world, especially among the least developed countries (LDC), which a list of the 50 most is depicted in Figure 1.3.

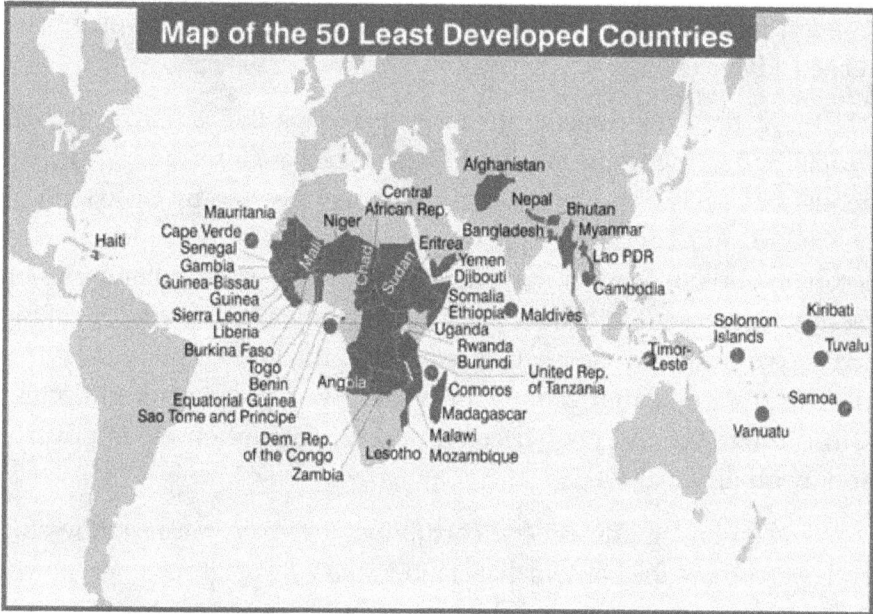

Figure 1.3 – The 50 least developed countries in the world. SOURCE: UNCTAD.

To identify corruption is not difficult, but it is harder to see the layers it can have, especially under the more formal, even legal forms of *corruption*. It is easy to assume that these formal forms are not even an issue because they are often part of the laws and institutions that govern national and international communities and many of us will be accustomed to it—it is how it works, so to speak. If a president of an emerging country gets paid a bribe and as a result taxes are reduced to benefit certain corporations or even markets, what do we, the general public, know?

Corruption promotes, and often determines, the misuse of governments' resources by diverting them from sectors of vital importance such as health, education and development. Hence, the people that have most needs, the poor people, are the ones deprived of economic growth and development opportunities, which in turn causes significant income inequalities and lack of social mobility. Corruption also siphons off goods and money intended to alleviate poverty. These leakages compromise a country's economic growth, investment levels, poverty reduction efforts and other development-related advances.

At the same time, petty corruption saps the resources of poor people by forcing them to offer bribes in exchange for access to basic goods and services — many of which may be free by law, such as healthcare and education. With few other choices, poor people may resort to corruption as a survival strategy to overcome the exclusion faced when trying to go to school, get a job, buy a house, vote or simply participate in their societies. Consequently, the cost of public services rises to the point that economically deprived people can no longer afford them. As the poor become poorer, corruption feeds poverty and inequality.

Combating poverty and corruption, therefore, means addressing and overcoming the barriers that stand in the way of citizen engagement and a state's accountability. While most emerging economies claim that the equal participation and rights of citizens exist, in reality they rarely apply to the poor. Hence, to be effective, pro-poor anti-corruption strategies must look more closely at the larger context that limits opportunities for poor citizens to participate in political, economic and social processes.

Political Participation and Accountability.

Corruption in the political sphere attracts growing attention in more and more countries covered by this report. The demand for the accountability of political leaders and the transparency of political parties has begun to trigger reform in those areas. Private business has also become a focus of anti-corruption reform: besides being object of state oversight, this sector has started its own initiatives to curb corruption.

Linking the rights of marginalized communities and individuals to more accountable governments is a fundamental first step for developing a pro-poor anti-corruption strategy. Citizens giving their governments the power to act on their behalf shape a country's policies. Corruption by public and private sector officials taints this process, distorts constitutions and institutions, and results in poverty and unequal development. By strengthening political accountability, policies ensure that the poor are seen not as victims but rather as stakeholders in the fight against corruption. For now, a consensus on how to strengthen these elements in practice seems to still remain elusive within development cooperation circles.[13]

Notwithstanding, despite large differences in the problems prevalent in the various countries and the existing remedies, recent efforts to prevent corruption target similar areas across the region. Most countries that have endorsed the OECD's Anti-Corruption Action Plan, for example, attribute an important role to administrative reform. Hence, the various strategies to prevent corruption address integrity, effective procedures and transparent rules.

The integrity and competence of public officials are fundamental prerequisites for a reliable and efficient public administration. Many countries in the region and beyond have thus adopted measures that aim to ensure integrity in the hiring and promoting of staff, provide adequate remuneration and set and implement clear rules of conduct for public officials.

Past and current efforts to reduce poverty suggests that corruption has been a constant obstacle for countries, particularly emerging economies, trying to bring about the political, economic and social changes desired for their development. Across different country contexts, corruption has been a cause and consequence of poverty. At the same time, as depicted in Figure 1.4, corruption is a by-product of poverty. The poorest countries in the world, already marginalized, tend to suffer a double level of exclusion in countries where corruption characterizes the rules of the game. Interesting enough, oil-producing countries are also in the list.

[13] OECD (2007) Overview by the DAC Chair, In Development Co-operation Report. Vol. 8(1), chapter 1 (Paris, France: OECD, 2007).

RANK	COUNTRY	SCORE
175	Somalia	8
175	North Korea	8
175	Afghanistan	8
174	Sudan	11
173	South Sudan	14
172	Libya	15
171	Iraq	16
168	Turkmenistan	17
168	Syria	17
168	Uzbekistan	17
167	Yemen	18
163	Equatorial Guinea	19
163	Chad	19
163	Haiti	19
163	Guinea Bissau	19
160	Cambodia	20
160	Eritrea	20
160	Venezuela	20

Figure 1.4 – The most corrupt countries in the world. SOURCE: Business Insider.

According to Transparency International[14] (TI), many of the emerging and frontier countries around the globe experience major challenges with corruption. Figure 1.5 provides a global picture of 2013 corruption scores according to Transparency International[15'] RiskRadar[16]. When we look at the BRICS (Brazil, Russia, India, China, and South Africa) countries, for example, Chinese firms have the weakest overall performance among this bloc of nations.

[14] http://www.transparency.org/country
[15] http://www.dw.com/image/0,,17266841_401,00.jpg
[16] The RiskRadar is a content platform for people who wish to keep abreast of the latest developments in AML and anti-bribery and corruption. The RiskRadar is powered by LexisNexis.

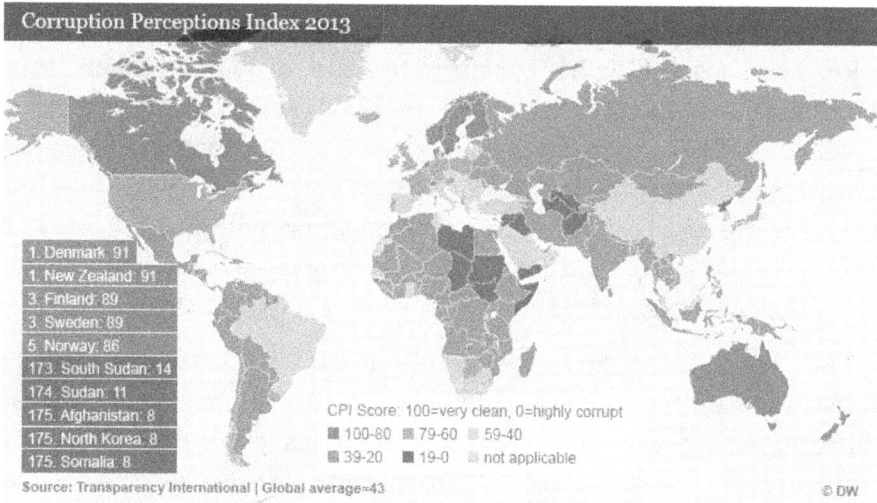

Figure 1.5 – 2013 Global Corruption Index. SOURCE: Transparency International

In its report titled *Transparency in Corporate Reporting: Assessing Emerging Market Multinationals*[17] TI analyzed 100 of the fastest growing companies based in 16 emerging markets. Three quarters of the businesses scored less than five out of 10, where zero is the least transparent. Scores were based on publicly available information about anti-corruption measures, transparency in reporting, how the companies structure themselves and the amount of financial information they provide for each country they operate in.

Chinese companies accounted for more than a third of the assessed businesses. According to TI China must take "immediate action"[18] to raise standards. Companies in India scored best out of the BRICS with a result of 5.4. The study said this was down to national laws obliging publication of key financial information on

[17] Kowalczyk-Hoyer, Barbara & Côté-Freeman, Susan (2013) Transparency in corporate reporting: Assessing emerging market multinationals, Transparency International, 10/16/2013,
http://transparency.org/whatwedo/pub/transparency_in_corporate_reporting_assessing_emerging_market_multinational, last accessed on 11/02/2013.

[18] Ibidem

subsidiaries. Some 75 of the 100 companies in the report come from BRICS nations, which have contributed 50% of world growth since the financial crisis. The study said about 60% of the firms evaluated does not disclose information about political contributions. TI called on companies in emerging markets to show the public what they are doing to prevent corruption and their relations with governments. It added legislation should be introduced to make companies publish what they pay to governments in every country where they operate.

To continue to foster consistent growth emerging markets must step up in playing their part in the global fight against corruption. As emerging market companies expand their global influence they should seize the opportunity to become active participants in the role of stopping corruption internationally.

Government infrastructure contracts in emerging and frontier markets in general, might be hard to access without breaking the FCPA or the 2011 UK Bribery Act, because requests for bribes are increasing in state procurement processes at both provincial and local government level. This can be a major problem for emerging and frontier market growth.

Fraud in the construction sector, according to Grant Thornton,[19] a global think-tank based in the UK, could be worth as much as $860 billion dollars globally, which is about 10 percent of industry revenues, and it could hit $1.5 trillion by 2025. Software and systems are a key element of the fight against fraud but the construction sector is a relatively low-level adopter of technology, while there would be more opportunities for wrongdoing as the economy recovers.

It is important to note, however, corruption is not only a challenge on emerging markets. Advanced economies are also plagued by it, either as a consideration of a cost for doing business in emerging markets or for accepting or being victims of extortions. Across Australia, Canada, India, the UK and the U.S. it is evident that fraud in the development of infrastructure is commonplace and in some cases endemic.

[19] http://www.grant-thornton.co.uk/

In the UK, the three biggest areas of construction fraud are bid rigging, alterations to contracts and false misrepresentation, which covers use of illegal workers, falsifying reports, results or certificates, and non-compliance with regulations. The Grant Thornton's report refers to *breakfast clubs*,[20] where contractors meet to decide who will win the latest contract. In New York, the think-tank calculated that 5 percent of the value of construction projects went to five Mafia families in 2011 alone.

The problem is that many companies are not aware of their increased levels of liability or the new legal risks that threaten their business. The drive for growth is also increasing corporate corruption risk as businesses expand into emerging markets where corruption tends to be more endemic. In countries such as the UK, Canada and Australia, the propensity of bid rigging has been normalized to the extent that it might be perceived as legal, according to Grant Thornton's report.

To prevent fraud, policymakers in emerging and frontier market countries need to combat the practice by making the issue a priority in its national agenda. It needs to devise processes to scrutinizing in-country multinational firms and their own corporations—in particularly; they should not forget to extend such scrutiny to its government agencies. Policymakers must be able, and capable, to place aside reputational issues and prosecute fraudsters. The use of information systems and technology, in an effort to tap onto big data to identify and predict fraud is also paramount. Governments must also encourage whistleblowing, and provide full support and cooperation to these practices listed here.

[20] Ibidem

Chapter 2 – A History of the FCPA

Historical Overview

The Foreign Corrupt Practices Act (FCPA) is a United States' federal law enacted in 1977, known primarily for two of its main provisions, one that addresses accounting transparency requirements under the Securities Exchange Act of 1934 and another concerning bribery of foreign officials.[21] The act was amended in 1988 and then again in 1998. As of 2012 there were continued congressional concerns, which is discussed in more detail later in this book.[22]

As with most new laws, the FCPA did not appear out of thin air. Rather, real events and policy reasons motivated Congress to enact the FCPA. The FCPA was enacted in the surge of public morality following the Watergate Scandal and in response to an U.S. congressional investigation uncovering widespread bribery among domestic companies operating overseas. Discovery of the foreign corporate payments problem in the mid-1970s resulted from a combination of work by the Office of the Watergate Special Prosecutor, including related follow-up work and investigations by

---

[21] Funk, T. Markus, "Getting What They Pay For: The Far-Reaching Impact Of the Dodd-Frank Act's 'Whistleblower Bounty' Incentives on FCPA Enforcement," White Collar Crime Report (Bureau of National Affairs) 5 (19): 1–3.

[22] LeRoy Miller, Roger (2011). Business Law Today: The Essentials. United States: South-Western Cengage Learning. p. 127. ISBN 1-133-19135-5.

the Securities and Exchange Commission (SEC) and Senator Frank Church's Subcommittee on Multinational Corporations (Church Committee).

The Report of the Securities and Exchange Commission on Questionable and Illegal Corporate Payments and Practices (SEC Report) stated as follows:

> In 1973, as a result of the work of the Office of the [Watergate] Special Prosecutor, several corporations and executive officers were charged with using corporate funds for illegal domestic political contributions. The Commission recognized that these activities involved matters of possible significance to public investors, the nondisclosure of which might entail violations of the federal securities laws. . . . The Commission's inquiry into the circumstances surrounding alleged illegal political campaign contributions revealed that violations of the federal securities laws had indeed occurred. The staff discovered falsifications of corporate financial records, designed to disguise or conceal the source and application of corporate funds misused for illegal purposes, as well as the existence of secret "slush funds" disbursed outside the normal financial accountability system. These secret funds were used for a number of purposes, including in some instances, questionable or illegal foreign payments. These practices cast doubt on the integrity and reliability of the corporate books and records, which are the very foundation of the disclosure system established by the federal securities laws.[23]

As evident from the SEC Report, the SEC's focus was not whether the discovered domestic and foreign payments were or should be per se illegal under U.S. law, but rather whether such payments were and should be disclosed to investors. Along with the SEC's work, the Church Committee also helped shine a light on questionable foreign corporate payments.[24] In May 1975, the Church

---

[23] U.S. Sec. & Exch. Comm'n, Report of The Securities and Exchange Commission on Questionable and Illegal Corporate Payments and Practices.

[24] Chaired by Senator Church, the Subcommittee on Multinational Corporations of the Senate Foreign Relations Committee was established in 1972, and among other things, this

Committee held the first of several hearings generally dealing with U.S. corporate political contributions to foreign governments. Senator Church opened the hearings as follows:

> In the course of the Watergate Committee hearings and the investigation by the Special Prosecutor, it became apparent that major American corporations had made illegal political contributions in the United States. More recently, the [SEC] has revealed that several multinational corporations had failed to report to their shareholders millions of dollars of offshore payments in violation of the Securities laws of the United States. . . .
>
> The [SEC] is understandably concerned that the disclosure requirements of U.S. laws are complied with. This subcommittee is concerned with the foreign policy consequences of these payments by U.S.-based multinational corporations.
>
> This is not a pleasant or easy subject for the corporations involved or U.S. Government officials to discuss in a public forum. This subcommittee deliberated long and hard as to whether it should pursue this matter, and, if so, in what fashion. It decided by a unanimous vote to initiate this investigation and to do so in open public hearings. For what we are concerned with is not a question of private or public morality. What concerns us here is a major issue of foreign policy for the United States.[25]

Through the mid-1970s, Congress held numerous hearings in the aftermath of news and disclosures of questionable foreign corporate payments to a variety of recipients and for a variety of

subcommittee investigated relationships between U.S. oil companies and Middle East producing nations, corporate plans to influence elections in Chile, and complicity between U.S. companies and other foreign countries. See generally RALPH W. HANSEN & DEBORAH J. ROBERTS, THE FRANK CHURCH PAPERS: A SUMMARY GUIDE (Boise State Univ. ed., 1988), available at http://libraries.boisestate.edu/special/church/church.shtm.

[25] Multinational Corporations and United States Foreign Policy: Hearings Before the Subcomm. on Multinational Corps. of the S. Comm. on Foreign Relations, 94th Cong. 1 (1975) (statement of Sen. Frank Church, Chairman, Subcomm. on Multinational Corps., S. Comm. on Foreign Relations) [hereinafter Multinational Corporations].

reasons.　The Church Committee sought answers to the following questions regarding the questionable payments:

> In what country were they made? Were they illegal in the country in which they were made? If the corporation was reluctant, did it bring the matter to the attention of the U.S. Embassy? If not, why not? Does the United States have a foreign assistance program in the country in which the payment was made? Did our Government's Overseas Private Investment Corporation guarantee the company's investment in the country, in whole or in part? Was the U.S. Embassy aware of such payments? If not, why not?[26]

Over the course of four months in 1975, the Church Committee held separate hearings, focusing in particularly on payments made by, among others, Lockheed Aircraft Corporation, Gulf Oil Corporation, Mobil Oil, United Brands Company, Northrop Corporation, Ashland Oil, and Exxon Corporation. Each of these corporations were the subject of allegations, or had already made admissions, concerning questionable payments made directly or indirectly to foreign government officials or foreign political parties in connection with a business purpose.

For instance, Gulf Oil principally involved contributions to the political campaign of the President of the Republic of Korea.[27] Northrop principally involved payments to a Saudi Arabian general.[28] Exxon principally involved contributions to Italian political parties.[29] Mobil Oil also principally involved contributions to Italian

---

[26] Ibidem, Id. at 2 (statement of Sen. Frank Church, Chairman, Subcomm. on Multinational Corps., S. Comm. on Foreign Relations).

[27] The Activities of American Multinational Corporations Abroad: Hearings Before the Subcomm. on Int'l Econ. Policy of the H. Comm. on Int'l Relations, 94th Cong. 2 (1975) (statement of Rep. Robert N. C. Nix, Chairman, Subcomm. on Int'l Econ. Policy, H. Comm. on Int'l Relations) [hereinafter American Multinational Corporations Abroad].

[28] Ibidem.

[29] See Multinational Corporations, supra note 4, at 239 (statement of Sen. Frank Church, Chairman, Subcomm. on Multinational Corps., S. Comm. on Foreign Relations).

political parties.[30] Lockheed principally involved payments to Japanese Prime Minister Tanaka, Prince Bernhard (the Inspector General of the Dutch Armed Forces and the husband of Queen Juliana of the Netherlands), and Italian political parties.[31] In addition, although not the focus of separate Church Committee hearings, foreign payments by United Brands and Ashland Oil also concerned Congress. United Brands principally involved payments to Oswaldo Lopez Arellano, the President of Honduras.[32]   Ashland Oil principally involved payments to Albert Bernard Bongo, the President of Gabon.[33]

The Lockheed scandal, in particular, prompted significant congressional concern given that during the time period the payments were made Lockheed was the recipient of a $250 million federal loan guarantee intended to keep the company out of bankruptcy. A Washington Post editorial included in the legislative record noted as follows:

> According to the New York Times, Kodama was the recipient of CIA funds for covert projects on several occasions. The Times also reports that the CIA was aware of Kodama's relationship with Lockheed from the late 1950s on. And it's well known that Lockheed has had a relationship with the CIA over the years.[34]

---

[30] See id. at 315 (statement of Everett Checket, Exec. Vice President, Int'l Div., Mobil Oil Corp).

[31] See Foreign Payments Disclosure: Hearings Before the Subcomm. on Consumer Prot. and Fin. of the H. Comm. on Interstate and Foreign Commerce, 94th Cong. 2 (1976) (statement of Rep. John M. Murphy, Chairman, Subcomm. on Consumer Prot. and Fin., H. Comm. on Interstate and Foreign Commerce) [hereinafter Foreign Payments Disclosure].

[32] See American Multinational Corporations Abroad, supra note 7, at 2 (statement of Rep. Robert N. C. Nix, Chairman, Subcomm. on Int'l Econ. Policy, H. Comm. on Int'l Relations).

[33] Ibidem.

[34] Foreign and Corporate Bribes: Hearings Before the S. Comm. on Banking, Hous., and Urban Affairs, 94th Cong. 46 (1976) (statement of Sen. William Proxmire, Chairman, S. Comm. on Banking, Hous., and Urban Affairs) [hereinafter Foreign and Corporate Bribes].

In 1975, the House held a series of hearings largely focused on whether the discovered payments were a violation of U.S. law. The primary focus of Congress's investigation was whether the existing securities laws, tax laws, and/or antitrust laws adequately addressed the foreign corporate payments problem. Early in Congress's investigation of the problem, SEC Chairman Garrett highlighted the potential deficiencies of the securities laws as a comprehensive solution to the problem.

Not only were the securities laws materiality threshold viewed as deficient in requiring disclosure of all corporate payments to foreign government officials, but congressional leaders were also surprised to learn that existing corporate record-keeping and internal control provisions were deficient as well. Upon discovery of the foreign corporate payments problem, Congress's first task was to determine if existing law adequately captured these payments. While certain existing laws did indirectly deal with various aspects of the problem, the prevailing view was that existing laws were deficient and that a new and direct legislative remedy was needed.

Congress soon discovered that these payments were not directly prohibited under U.S. law, even if certain existing laws, such as tax and securities disclosure laws, were possibly indirectly implicated. In concluding his opening remarks, Senator Church stated as follows: "In short, we cannot close our eyes to this problem. It is no longer sufficient to simply sigh and say that is the way business is done. It is time to treat the issue for what it is: a serious foreign policy problem."[35]

Congress set out to close this gap. In the mid-1970s, Congress journeyed into uncharted territory. There was concern that enacting a law governing business interactions with foreign government officials in foreign lands would be viewed as the U.S. legislating morality and that such a law might be resented abroad. Even though many of the foreign corporate payments presented a moral quandary, not all participants in the legislative debate were prepared

[35] Ibidem.

to offer a firm response. For instance, during a Senate hearing in 1975 focused on the Lockheed scandal, Senator John Tower stated: "A central question is raised here and that is, is it morally right for an American company to operate within the mores and folkways of the society in which they are trying to do business? I'm not prepared to give a snap answer to that myself."[36]

[36] Lockheed Bribery: Hearings Before the S. Comm on Banking, Hous., and Urban Affairs, 94th Cong. 12 (1975) (statement of Sen. John Tower, Member, S. Comm. On Banking, Hous., and Urban Affairs) [hereinafter Lockheed Bribery].

Chapter 3 – The FCPA Fundamentals

Overview

As discussed in chapter 2, Congress enacted the FCPA to bring a halt to the bribery of foreign officials and to restore public confidence in the integrity of the American business system. The Act was signed into law by President Jimmy Carter on December 19, 1977, and amended in 1998 by the International Anti-Bribery Act of 1998, which was designed to implement the anti-bribery conventions of the OECD. The FCPA makes it a crime for any American citizen and businesses to bribe foreign public officials for business purposes. It also imposes certain accounting standards on public U.S. companies.

Developing and enacting it was not a straightforward process, as also outlined in chapter two. The foreign corporate payments that were discovered from several companies were not the simple and safe issue they appeared to be at first blush. Congress encountered many difficult and complex issues as it considered solutions including the foreign business conditions in which certain of the payments were made, whether unilateral U.S. action would put companies at a competitive disadvantage, and the basic issue of defining bribery.

As depicted in Figure 3.1, it is very important that multinationals corporations, especially those engaging with foreign government projects and officials, develop a good understanding of the Act, to protect themselves, their staff, reputation, and business practices.

FCPA – Foreign Corrupt Practices Act

- Protect your business and reputation
- Understand what the law and regulation require of you
- Understand the risks posed by corrupt customers
- Identify the customers who are higher risk

Figure 3.1 – Top reasons to be trained and have full understanding of the FCPA

Between June 1975 and September 1977, approximately twenty bills were introduced in the Senate or the House during the 94th or 95th Congresses to address the foreign corporate payments problem.[37] For instance, H.R. 7539, introduced by Representative Solarz in June 1975 during the middle of the Church Committee hearings, was the first bill to address the problem which sought "[t]o give the Secretary of State responsibility for monitoring the overseas business activities of American companies in order to detect any violations of [f]ederal law and to make it unlawful for an American company to bribe any foreign official."[38]

Moreover, despite unanimous passage of Senate Resolution 265, the Ford administration opposed introducing the complex payments problem into already difficult trade negotiations. Travis

[37] Declaration of Prof. Michael J. Koehler in Support of Defendants' Motion to Dismiss Counts One Through Ten of the Indictment at 9, United States v. Carson, No. SACR 09- 0007-JVS (C.D. Cal. Sept. 20, 2011).

[38] H.R. 7539, 94th Cong. (1975).

Reed, then Assistant Secretary of Commerce for Domestic and International Business, stated that trade negotiations involved a very large number of countries not all of which necessarily shared the U.S. interest in a code of conduct concerning unethical payments. Consequently, Reed argued, if this problem were introduced only into the multilateral trade negotiations, it would might not receive the degree of support and attention necessary to reach an effective agreement. In his opinion, the industrialized exporting countries in which most multinational corporations were based and with which the U.S. could realistically expect to reach an effective agreement constituted a relatively small portion of the total participants.

Reed suggested that the Organization for Economic Cooperation and Development (OECD), a group consisting of the major industrialized nations, would provide a "proper vehicle . . . to attempt to get some unanimity of thought in regard to how this universal code of conduct would be accepted and could then be introduced into the General Agreement on Tariffs and Trade (GATT) or any other appropriate body."[39]

Notwithstanding the many difficult and complex issues Congress encountered, it proceeded to seek legislative remedies to the foreign corporate payments problem. Congress sought to address the problem from a variety of angles, which resulted on two main competing legislative responses, a disclosure approach as to a broad category of payments, and a criminalization approach as to a narrow category of payments. Despite significant minority concern, the FCPA adopted a criminalization approach as it was viewed as more effective in deterring improper payments and less burdensome on business.

After more than two years of investigation, deliberation and consideration of the foreign corporate payments problem and the policy ramifications of such payments, and despite divergent views as to the problem and the difficult and complex issues presented,

---

[39] Protecting U.S. Trade Abroad, supra note 22, at 31–32 (statement of Travis Reed, Assistant U.S. Sec'y of Commerce, Domestic and Int'l Bus. Admin.).

Congress completed its pioneering journey and passed the first law in the world governing domestic business conduct with foreign government officials in foreign markets. Speaking on the House floor on December 7, 1977, Representative Eckhardt summed up the journey and stated that the FCPA was "one of the more important pieces of legislation to be considered by the Congress this year."[40]

The FCPA was a pioneering statute. Yet at the same time, the FCPA was intended to be a limited statute. Even though Congress was aware of a wide range of foreign corporate payments to a variety of recipients for a variety of reasons, it intended, and accepted in passing the FCPA, to capture only a narrow category of such payments. Among other things, Congress limited the FCPA's payment provisions to a narrow category of foreign recipients and further narrowed the range of actionable payments to those involving foreign government procurement or to influence foreign government legislation or regulations. In addition, Congress chose not to capture so-called facilitation payments given the difficult and complex business conditions encountered in many foreign markets.

As evident from the legislative activity discussed above, despite learning of a wide range of foreign corporate payments, Congress limited the FCPA's payment provisions to a narrow category of foreign recipients and further narrowed the range of actionable payments to those involving foreign government procurement or to influence foreign government legislation or regulations. Congressional intent on these issues is further evidenced by the recipient categories in the FCPA and the law's business purpose test as to prohibited payments.

FCPA Purpose and Requirements

The FCPA's purpose is to make it unlawful for certain classes of persons and entities to make payments to foreign government officials to assist in obtaining or retaining business. It applies to any act by U.S. businesses, foreign corporations trading securities in the

---

[40] 123 CONG. REC. 38,778 (1977) (statement of Rep. Bob Eckhardt).

U.S., American nationals, citizens, and residents acting in furtherance of a foreign corrupt practice whether or not they are physically present in the U.S. This is considered the nationality principle of the act.

In other words, the FCPA makes it illegal for companies and their supervisors to influence anyone with any personal payments or rewards[41]. The FCPA defines "foreign official" to mean

> any officer or employee of a foreign government or any department, agency, or instrumentality thereof, or any person acting in an official capacity for or on behalf of such government or department, agency or instrumentality. Such term does not include any employee of a foreign government or any department, agency, or instrumentality thereof whose duties are essentially ministerial or clerical.[42]

As argued by Alexandro Posadas,[43] of Duke University, the Act governs not only payments to "foreign officials," but also to candidates, and parties, as well as any other recipient if part of the bribe is ultimately attributable to a foreign official, candidate, or party. These payments are not restricted to just monetary forms and may include anything of value.[44] The meaning of foreign official, however, is broad.

For example, an owner of a bank who is also the minister of finance would be considered as a foreign official according to the

[41] Luthans, Fred; Doh, Jonathan (2014). International Management Culture, Strategy, and Behavior (9th ed.). New York, NY: McGraw-Hill Education. ISBN 978-0-07-786244-2.

[42] See Foreign Corrupt Practices Act of 1977, Pub. L. No. 95-213, § 102, 91 Stat. 1494, 1496, amended by Foreign Corrupt Practices Act Amendments of 1988, Pub. L. No. 100- 418, tit. V, subtit. A, pt. 1, 102 Stat. 1415 and by International Anti-Bribery and Fair Competition Act of 1998, Pub. L. No. 105-366, 112 Stat. 3302 (codified as amended in scattered sections of 15 U.S.C.) (emphasis added).

[43] Posadas, Alejandro (2000) Combating Corruption Under International Law, 10 Duke University Journal of Comparative and International Law pages 345-414, http://scholarship.law.duke.edu/djcil/vol10/iss2/4, last accessed 12/02/2013.

[44] Ibidem

U.S. government. Doctors at government-owned or managed hospitals are also considered to be foreign officials under the FCPA, as is anyone working for a government-owned or managed institution or enterprise. Employees of international organizations such as the United Nations are also considered to be foreign officials under the FCPA.

Whenever businesses decide to follow the unethical road, there are consequences including high financial penalties. Any individuals that are involved in those activities may face prison time.[45] This act was passed to make it unlawful for certain classes of persons and entities to make payments to foreign government officials to assist in obtaining or retaining business. In the case of foreign natural and legal persons, the Act covers their deeds if they are in the U.S. at the time of the corrupt conduct. This is considered the protective principle of the act.

More specifically, the FCPA's anti-bribery provisions prohibit the willful use of the mails or any means of instrumentality of interstate commerce corruptly in furtherance of any offer, payment, promise to pay, or authorization of the payment of money or anything of value to any person, while knowing that all or a portion of such money or thing of value will be offered, given or promised, directly or indirectly, to a foreign official to influence the foreign official in his or her official capacity, induce the foreign official to do or omit to do an act in violation of his or her lawful duty, or to secure any improper advantage in order to assist in obtaining or retaining business for or with, or directing business to, any person.

The FCPA's definition of "foreign official," however, does not include many payment recipient categories Congress learned of during its investigation. For instance, and as stated above, Congress learned of a number of questionable foreign commercial payments, including those made to induce a nongovernment customer's purchasing decisions. However, Congress chose not to capture

---

[45] Ibidem.

payments to such recipients in its definition of "foreign official" or otherwise in the FCPA.

Moreover, Congress further narrowed the term "foreign official" by capturing only traditional foreign government officials performing official or public functions, except officials whose duties were essentially ministerial or clerical as stated above.[46] The legislative record evidences that Congress was aware of the existence of so-called state-owned or state-controlled enterprises (SOEs) and that some of the questionable payments uncovered or disclosed may have involved such entities.

The anti-bribery provisions of the FCPA have applied, since 1977, to all U.S. persons and certain foreign issuers of securities. With the enactment of certain amendments in 1998, the anti-bribery provisions of the FCPA now also apply to foreign firms and persons who cause, directly or through agents, an act in furtherance of such a corrupt payment to take place within the territory of the United States.

Companies whose securities are listed in the United States are also required by the FCPA to meet its accounting provisions. These accounting provisions, which were designed to operate in tandem with the anti-bribery provisions of the FCPA, require corporations covered by the provisions to:

1. Make and keep books and records that accurately and fairly reflect the transactions of the corporation and
2. Devise and maintain an adequate system of internal accounting controls.

---

[46] For more on the legislative history concerning "foreign official," see Declaration of Professor Michael J. Koehler in Support of Defendants' Motion to Dismiss Counts One Through Ten of the Indictment, United States v. Carson, No. SACR 09-0007-JVS (C.D. Cal. Feb. 21, 2011), available at http://www.scribd.com/doc/49310598/U-S-v-Stuart-Carson-elal- Declaration-of-Professor-Michael-Koehler.

Whether observed internally by an FCPA compliance officer or externally in the actions of a business partner, the following circumstances raise flags that should trigger an investigation into whether the FCPA is implicated:

- Unusually large commissions, retainers or fees
- Information suggesting questionable reputation of business partner
- Refusal to make FCPA-related representations
- Unusual methods of payments
- Promises of business by or from a government official
- Family or business relationship with a government official
- Business partner lacking adequate facilities or ability to provide promised results
- Payment of contingent fees
- Making of political contributions
- Conduct prohibited under local law

In summary, all individuals subject to the FCPA include any U.S. or foreign corporation that has a class of securities registered (public trade companies), or that is required to file reports under the Securities and Exchange (SEC) Act of 1934.

FCPA Enforcement

The Securities and Exchange Commission (SEC) and the Department of Justice (DOJ) are both responsible for enforcing the FCPA. This is because the FCPA both amends an SEC Act and the criminal code. The SEC enforces the Act for companies it regulates and the Department of Justice enforces the bill regarding all other domestic companies.

Figure 3.2 shows the number of FCPA enforcement actions initiated by the statute's dual enforcers during each of the past ten years. As these figures bear out, the dedicated professionals at DOJ and the SEC (now numbering more than 60) have aggressively and successfully pursued their enforcement mandate in 2013 and recent years past.

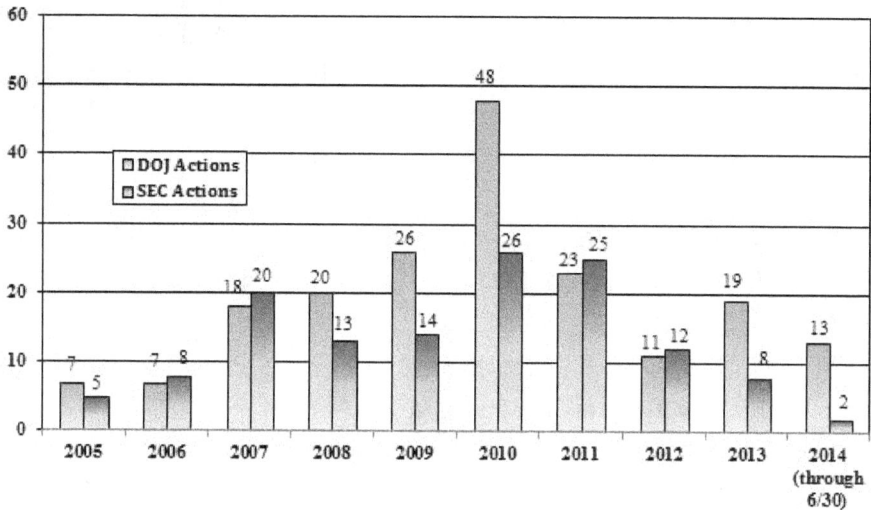

Figure 3.2 – FCPA enforcements during 2004-2014. SOURCE: Gibson Dunn[47]

This split was criticized even before the act was passed.[48] In 2010 the SEC created a specialized unit for FCPA enforcement.[49] In 2012, the SEC and the DOJ issued their first joint guide to the FCPA, a comprehensive tome of 120 pages; the Guide largely reiterates the agencies' longstanding enforcement principles.

Even so, the Guide promises to be a tremendously useful tool because it collects and rationalizes prior enforcement decisions and provides detailed guidance and hypotheticals in a number of areas. Moreover, the fact that the Guide was issued jointly is an important reassurance that the agencies have adopted, a unified approach to

[47] http://www.gibsondunn.com/publications/pages/2013-Year-End-FCPA-Update.aspx

[48] House Committee on Interstate and Foreign Commerce (September 28, 1977). "H.R. Rep. 95-640 REPORT together with MINORITY VIEWS To accompany H.R.3815" (PDF). Retrieved 22 February 2015.

[49] "SEC Names New Specialized Unit Chiefs and Head of New Office of Market Intelligence" (Press release). SEC. January 13, 2010. Retrieved 23 February 2015.

FCPA enforcement.[50]

The average closing cost for a corporate FCPA resolution, inclusive of DOJ and SEC fines, penalties, disgorgement, and prejudgment interest, was more than $80 million in 2013. That is a nearly fourfold increase over 2012. And looking at the horizon of cases to come while speaking at the 2013 American Conference Institute FCPA Conference ("ACI FCPA Conference"), DOJ's FCPA Unit Chief said that he expects DOJ to bring more "top 10 quality type cases" in 2014.

Among the ten FCPA-related enforcement actions involving corporations is the resolution of a non-FCPA but bribery-related disposition against BAE, which constituted the third largest foreign bribery-related case to date in terms of penalties. The United States and United Kingdom imposed a combined penalty on BAE of over $445 million, most of which, $400 million, was charged by the DOJ.

The SEC imposed a combined FCPA-related monetary penalty of $185 million on carmaker Daimler AG, the fourth largest such penalty since the FCPA's enactment in 1977. With companies such as Technip, fined 245 Million Euros (about $326.8 million dollars, ENI fined 250 Million Euros, about $333.5 million dollars, Pride fined $56.2 million dollars and Alcatel-Lucent $137.4 million dollars, announcing or reserving funds for anticipated settlements with the DOJ and the SEC, significant penalties may become the norm, rather than the exception. Figure 3.3 details the ten highest FCPA-related combined penalties imposed on corporations since enactment of the FCPA.

[50] Criminal Division of the U.S. Department of Justice and the Enforcement Division of the U.S. Securities and Exchange Commission (November 14, 2012). "A Resource Guide to the U.S. Foreign Corrupt Practices Act." p. 130. Retrieved 23 February 2015.

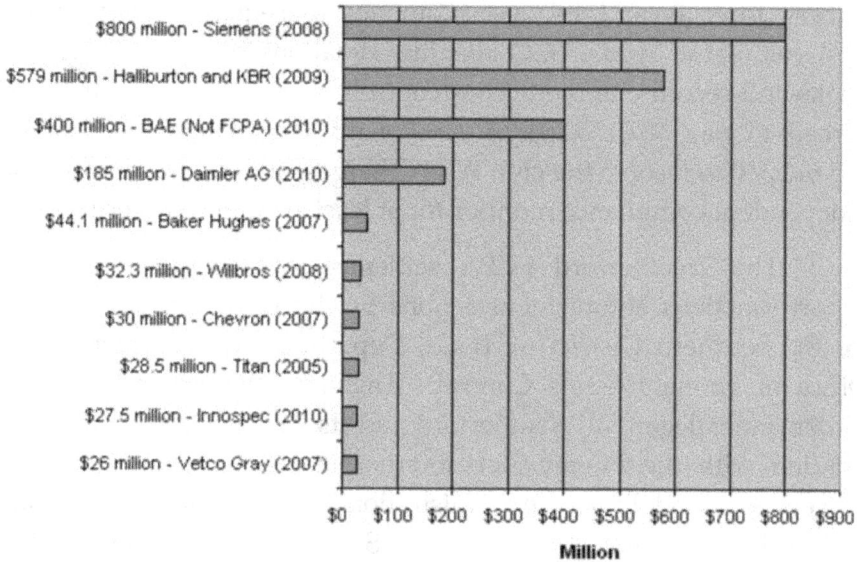

Figure 3.3 – Largest FCPA settlement in terms of combined penalties. SOURCE: Miller Chevalier[51]

Two of the nine corporate FCPA resolutions of 2013, the French oil and gas company Total, S.A. and Weatherford International Ltd., joined the infamous "FCPA Top 10" list. Total settled on $398.2 million for alleged corruption in Iran. With respect to Weatherford, DOJ and the SEC announced a joint FCPA resolution with the Swiss oil services firm on November 26, 2013. According to the charging documents, between 2002 and 2011 Weatherford, through its subsidiaries and third-party representatives, made corrupt payments to obtain or retain business in six foreign countries including Albania, Algeria, Angola, Congo, Iraq, and another, unnamed Middle Eastern country.

To resolve the charges, Weatherford entered into a deferred prosecution agreement (DPA) with DOJ for a single alleged violation of the internal controls provision. Simultaneously, a Bermudan subsidiary pleaded guilty to one count of violating the FCPA's anti-

[51]

http://www.millerchevalier.com/Publications/MillerChevalierPublications?find=30601

bribery provision and the parent company consented to the filing of a civil complaint by the SEC alleging violations of the anti-bribery, books-and-records, and internal controls provisions. Weatherford agreed to pay $87,178,256 to resolve the criminal FCPA charges, $65,612,360 to resolve the civil FCPA charges, and agreed to retain an independent compliance monitor for at least an 18-month term.

The Weatherford FCPA settlement was coordinated with export sanctions enforcement actions by the U.S. Attorney's Office for the Southern District of Texas, Department of Commerce, and Office of Foreign Assets Control. Together, the export sanctions settlements allege that Weatherford and its subsidiaries violated the Trading with the Enemy Act, International Emergency Economic Powers Act, and Export Administration Regulations in connection with sales to Cuba, Iran, Mexico, Syria, and Venezuela. The sanctions side of the coordinated resolution resulted in a separate parent company DPA, two more subsidiary guilty pleas, $50 million in criminal fines, and a $50 million administrative penalty. Gibson Dunn[52], an international practice law firm known for excellence in the practice of law and expertise in FCPA cases, represented Weatherford in both the FCPA and sanctions settlements.

Given the consistent, public emphasis the SEC/DOJ have placed on the prosecution of individuals, including the suggestion that to receive "full cooperation credit" companies under investigation must identify and produce specific evidence of alleged individual culpability, as shown in Figure 3.4, one might expect 2016 to feature an uptick in the number of individuals charged. The SEC continues to rely on expanded authority under the 2010 Dodd-Frank Wall Street Reform and Consumer Protection Act to prosecute FCPA-related misconduct via administrative proceedings rather than through court-filed civil complaint.

[52] http://www.gibsondunn.com/about/Pages/default.aspx

Increase in DOJ and SEC Enforcement Activity Against Individuals

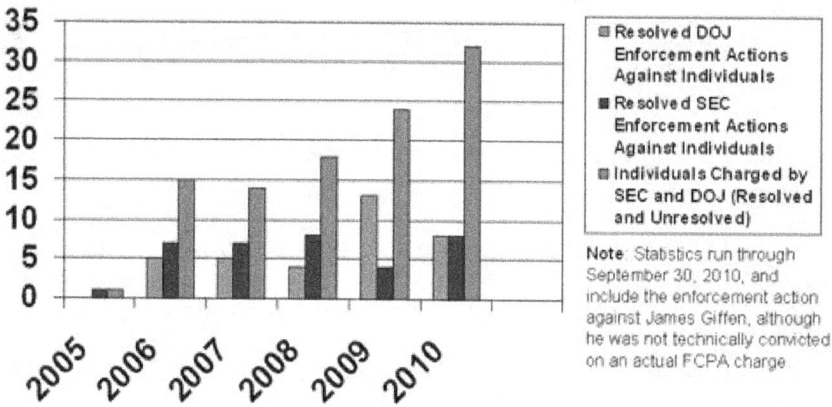

Figure 3.4 – FCPA enforcements on individuals 2005-2010. SOURCE: Miller Chevalier[53]

A summary of the FCPA, titled *FCPA Pocket Handbook* can be found at the end of this book, in Appendix A. The handbook provides all the main aspects one should be aware of regarding the FCPA. For a full copy of the FCPA, along with SEC and DOJ joined developed guidelines for compliance check *A Resource Guide to the U.S. Foreign Corrupt Practices Act*. This guide, a 130 pages free of charge resource, was developed by the Criminal Division of the U.S. Department of Justice and the Enforcement Division of the U.S. Securities and Exchange Commission. It can be accessed and downloaded from the Department of Justice website at www.justice.gov/criminal/fraud/fcpa or at the Securities and Exchange Commission website at www.sec.gov/spotlight/fcpa.shtml.

A Word about World Bank Enforcements

The World Bank is a consortium of two international banking institutions that together provide loans to developing countries for capital programs with the official goal of eradicating extreme poverty and hunger worldwide. In fiscal year 2013, the World Bank's two

---

[53] http://www.millerchevalier.com/portalresource/IncreaseinDOJandSEC

member institutions committed $31.5 billion in loans, grants, and guarantees. With the mammoth size of its international footprint, the World Bank has the ability to wield, and has wielded, its influence to become a leader in the global fight against corruption. As stated recently by World Bank Group President Jim Yong Kim, "Let's not mince words: in the developing world, corruption is Public Enemy Number 1. We will never tolerate corruption and I pledge to do all in our power to build upon our strong fight against it."

The World Bank's commitment to fighting corruption has been more than just rhetoric. In fiscal year 2013, the World Bank publicly debarred 47 entities and their affiliates found to have engaged in illegal practices. The impact of a World Bank debarment can be significant and long-lasting as long as 10 years as demonstrated by the recent high-profile sanctions against a Canadian engineering company for alleged corruption in Algeria, Bangladesh, Cambodia, and Libya.

Beyond the bar on participating in Bank-financed projects, a World Bank debarment can lead to significant collateral consequences, including cross-debarment by other multilateral development banks, government contracting authorities, and referrals to law enforcement authorities. Indeed, according to the 2013 annual report from the Integrity Vice Presidency, the World Bank's investigatory arm, 10 referrals from the Bank in the past fiscal year led to criminal investigations by national authorities. In addition, to get out of the debarment "penalty box," the Bank routinely requires companies to strengthen their compliance programs and to engage compliance monitors.

In light of the significant impact of its debarment processes on international businesses, the Work Bank has taken the laudable step of evaluating its sanctions system for potential refinement. The first phase of this "stock-taking" exercise, which ran from July through October 2013, involved consultations with multiple external stakeholders, including academics, debarment officials, and law firms that participate in World Bank proceedings, including Gibson Dunn. Notable reforms under consideration based on the recommendations of the U.S. defense bar included the following:

- Ensuring that legal counsel are able to participate in INT witness interviews;
- Ensuring that exculpatory and mitigating evidence is made available to the defense in sanctions proceedings;
- Increasing the proportionality between penalties and the underlying misconduct, and relying more on non-debarment sanctions, such as letters of reprimand;
- Considering collateral consequences in the sanctioning process;
- Using a more targeted approach to sanctioning corporate groups;
- Articulating standards by which the Bank will determine the need for external monitors, and establishing criteria for selecting monitors;
- Permitting settlements on a "no contest" basis rather than requiring an admission of wrongdoing; and
- Incentivizing voluntary disclosure and cooperation.

Chapter 4 - FCPA Violations and Actions

Overview

As discussed in earlier chapters, corruption poses significant legal and economic risks for companies conducting business around the world. The Department of Justice (DOJ) and the Securities and Exchange Commission (SEC) are jointly responsible for investigating, settling and prosecuting violations of the FCPA.

Beware. As more U.S. based companies, and individuals, seek to do business in foreign markets, they need to know that what is acceptable and commonplace elsewhere may be a violation of U.S. law. As discussed earlier, the FCPA, § 15 U.S.C. 78, et seq., makes it unlawful for U.S. persons and businesses, and certain foreign issuers of securities, to make a payment to a foreign official for the purpose of obtaining or retaining business for or with, or directing business to, any person.

Companies, which operate directly or through affiliated or unaffiliated parties, particularly in emerging and frontier economies, may be vulnerable to FCPA enforcement and should take steps to ensure compliance. Figure 4.1 provides some examples of FCPA violations focused on the payments of bribes to customs officials.

Paying Bribes to Customs Officials

In 2010, a global freight forwarding company and six of its corporate customers in the oil and gas industry resolved charges that they paid bribes to customs officials. The companies bribed customs officials in more than ten countries in exchange for such benefits as:

- evading customs duties on imported goods

- improperly expediting the importation of goods and equipment

- extending drilling contracts and lowering tax assessments

- obtaining false documentation related to temporary import permits for drilling rigs

- enabling the release of drilling rigs and other equipment from customs officials

In many instances, the improper payments at issue allowed the company to carry out its existing business, which fell within the FCPA's prohibition on corrupt payments made for the purpose of "retaining" business. The seven companies paid a total of more than $235 million in civil and criminal sanctions and disgorgement.

Figure 4.1 - Some examples of FCPA violations focused on the payments of bribes to customs officials.

Violations and Actions

Within the past decade, enforcement of the FCPA has been a top priority for U.S. enforcement agencies. The SEC has actually increased the level of FCPA actions, as shown in Figure 4.2, from seventeen cases in 2007 to twenty cases in 2011.

FCPA Actions Brought By The SEC

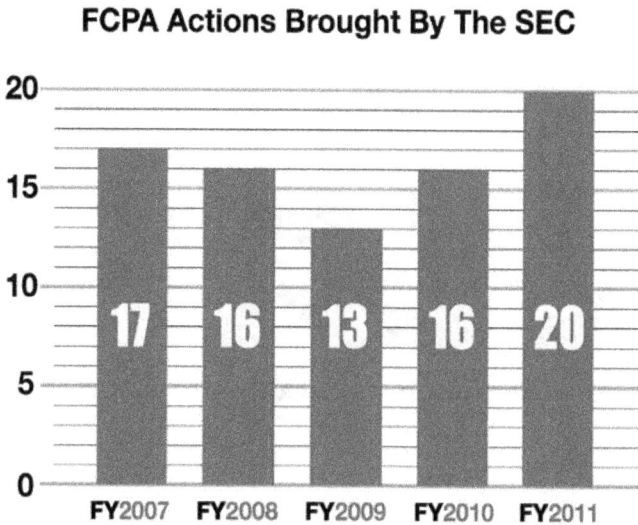

Figure 4.2 – FCPA actions brought by the SEC between 2007-2011. SOURCE: SEC

In turn, the DOJ, as depicted in Figure 4.3, has also ramped up the enforcement of the FCPA against individuals. In 2005, less than five individuals were prosecuted, but by 2010 more than 22 individuals were charged with violation. As an example, the former U.S. representative William J. Jefferson, democrat of Louisiana, was charged with violating the FCPA by bribing African governments for business interests.[54]

---

[54] Stout, David, 06/08/2009, "Ex-Rep. Jefferson Convicted in Bribery Scheme", The New York Times. p. A14, http://www.nytimes.com/2009/08/06/us/06jefferson.html, last accessed on 06/14/2013.

Increase in DOJ Enforcement
Against Individuals

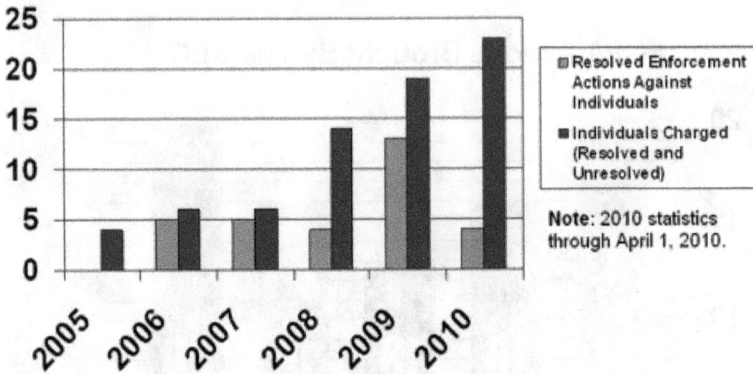

Legend:
- Resolved Enforcement Actions Against Individuals
- Individuals Charged (Resolved and Unresolved)

Note: 2010 statistics through April 1, 2010.

Figure 4.3 – Increase in DOJ enforcement of FCPA against individuals between 2005-2010.
SOURCE: DOJ

Within the past decade, enforcement of the FCPA has been a top priority for U.S. enforcement agencies. Stronger DOJ and SEC enforcement has increased the prominence of the FCPA from 2010 onwards.[55] The SEC website shows a complete list of enforcement cases since 1978. In 2014 alone, the DOJ initiated 24 prosecutions and the SEC opened eight enforcement actions. In recent years, the DOJ and the SEC have continued to push for strong enforcement against both companies and individuals who violate the FCPA and are imposing large penalties.

As depicted in Figure 4.4, some notable examples of FCPA violations include but are not limited to multinational corporations such as Walmart, BAE Systems, Baker Hughes, Daimler AG, Halliburton, KBR, Lucent Technologies, Monsanto, Siemens, Titan Corporation, Triton Energy Limited, Avon Products, and Invision Technologies.

---

[55] T. Markus Funk, "Another Landmark Year: 2010 FCPA Enforcement Year-in-Review and Trends for 2011," Bloomberg Law Reports (January 3, 2010).

Eight of the 10 largest settlements for violations of the
Foreign Corrupt Practices Act occurred in 2010.

	Penalty (in $ mil.)	Company	Company's headquarters	Year penalty was assessed
1.	$800	Siemens	Germany	2008
2.	$579	KBR/Halliburton	United States	2009
3.	$400	BAE Systems	United Kingdom	2010
4.	$365	ENI S.p.A/Snamprogetti Netherlands B.V.	Italy/Holland	2010
5.	$338	Technip S.A.	France	2010
6.	$185	Daimler AG	Germany	2010
7.	$137	Alcatel-Lucent	France	2010
8.	$82	Panalpina	Switzerland	2010
9.	$58	ABB Ltd.	Switzerland	2010
10.	$56	Pride International	United States	2010

Source: Hogan Lovells

Figure 4.4 - FCPA Enforcement: Billion-Dollar Fines and Jail Time. SOURCE: Hogan Lovells

Other notable select cases of the application of FCPA since 2008 include companies such as Biomet, Bizjet, Hewlett Packard Company, KBR, Marubeni Corporation, News Corporation, Siemens, Smith & Nephew and Walmart de Mexico. More recent notable cases include:

- **Siemens AG** – In 2008, the company paid a $450 million fine for violating the FCPA. This is one of the largest penalties ever collected by the DOJ for an FCPA case.[56]
- **Marubeni Corporation** - In 2012, this Japanese firm paid a criminal penalty of US$54.6 million for FCPA violations when

---

[56] Administrator. "Foreign Corrupt Practices Act Reporting Center - Siemens AG pays $450 million to settle FCPA bribery charges". foreign-corrupt-practices-act.org.

acting as an agent of the TKSJ joint venture, which comprised Technip, Snamprogetti Netherlands B.V., Kellogg Brown & Root Inc., and JGC Corporation. Between 1995 and 2004, the joint venture won four contracts in Nigeria worth more than US$6 billion, as a direct result of having paid US$51 million to Marubeni to be used to bribe Nigerian government officials.[57]

- **Smith & Nephew** - In 2012 the company paid US$22.2 million to the DOJ and SEC, and Bizjet International Sales and Support Inc. paid US$11.8 million to the DOJ for bribery of foreign government officials. Both companies entered into a deferred prosecution agreement.[58]

- **Biomet Inc.** - In March 2012, the company paid a criminal fine of US$17.3 million to resolve charges of FCPA violations and US$5.5 million in disgorgement of profits and pre-judgment interest to the SEC.[59]

- **Marubeni Corporation** - In March 2014 the company, again, agreed with the DOJ to pay a US$88 million fine after pleading guilty to taking part in a scheme to pay bribes to high ranking Indonesian officials in order to secure a lucrative power project.[60]

- **Goodyear Tire and Rubber Company** - On February 24, 2015, Goodyear agreed to pay more than $16 million to settle FCPA charges that two of its African subsidiaries allegedly paid $3.2 million in bribes that generated $14,122,535 in illicit profits.[61] The SEC FCPA charges involved Goodyear subsidiaries in

---

[57] US Department of Justice (17 January 2012). "Marubeni Corporation Resolves Foreign Corrupt Practices Act Investigation and Agrees to Pay a $54.6 Million Criminal Penalty".

[58] Smith & Nephew (6 February 2012). "Smith & Nephew reaches settlement with US Government". Smith & Nephew.

[59] Richard L. Cassin (26 March 2012). "Biomet Pays $22.8 Million To Settle Bribe Charges". The FCPA Blog.

[60] Brown, Howard. "$88 Million Fine Agreed by Marubeni Corporation of Japan with the U.S. Department of Justice to Settle a Foreign Corrupt Practices Act Investigation".

[61] Pelletier, Paul; Tidman, Aaron; Haviland, Jane (25 February 2015). "Goodyear's Settlement with the SEC Emphasizes the Importance of FCPA Due Diligence in M&A Transactions and of Having a Robust Anti-Corruption Policy". Mintz, Levin, Cohn, Ferris, Glovsky and Popeo, P.C. Retrieved 2 March 2015.

Kenya and Angola for allegedly paying bribes to government and private-sector workers in exchange for sales in each country.[62] According to the SEC because "Goodyear did not prevent or detect these improper payments because it failed to implement adequate FCPA compliance controls at its subsidiaries" and, for the Kenyan subsidiary, "because it failed to conduct adequate due diligence" prior to its acquisition. It was not alleged that Goodyear had any involvement with or knowledge of its subsidiaries' improper conduct.[63]

- **Alcoa World Alumina LLC:**[64] In January 2014, Alcoa's subsidiaries paid over US$110 million in bribes to Bahraini officials to influence negotiations with a government operated aluminum plant. Alcoa ended up paying a total of US$384 million to settle the case with the SEC and the DOJ. The SEC found that Alcoa did not conduct due diligence or otherwise seek to determine whether there was a legitimate business purpose for the use of a middleman in Bahrain, who was paying bribes on behalf of Alcoa to Bahraini government officials. This case constituted the fifth largest FCPA settlement in history.

- **Avon Products Inc.:**[65] In December 2014, Avon agreed to pay US$135 million to settle charges that it had failed to establish controls to detect and prevent US$8 million worth of payments and gifts from a subsidiary's employees and consultants to Chinese government officials. Avon was required to retain an independent compliance monitor to review its FCPA compliance program for a period of 18

[62] Horn, George (1 March 2015). "M and A Due Diligence Failures: FCPA and Goodyear". The National Law Review (Barnes & Thornburg LLP). Retrieved 2 March 2015.

[63] Mandelker, Sigal P.; Emert, Rochelle H.; Caraballo-Garrison, Phillip J. (27 February 2015). "Goodyear Pays for Sins of Subsidiaries in $16 Million Settlement". Proskauer Rose LLP. Retrieved 2 March 2015.

[64] SEC Charges Alcoa with FCPA Violations, January 9, 2014 at http://www.sec.gov/News/PressRelease/Detail/PressRelease/1370540596936#.VOzm_1 Uo5ow.

[65] SEC Charges Avon with FCPA Violations, December 17, 2014 at http://www.sec.gov/news/pressrelease/2014-285.html#.VOznFVUo5ow.

months, followed by an 18- month period of self-reporting on its compliance efforts. In reaching the settlement amount, the SEC considered Avon's cooperation and significant remedial measures.

- **Goodyear Tire & Rubber Company:**[66] In February 2015, Goodyear paid over US$16 million to settle SEC charges that it violated the FCPA when its subsidiaries paid bribes to land tire sales in Kenya and Angola. Goodyear was also required to report its FCPA remediation efforts to the SEC for a three-year period. The settlement reflects Goodyear's self-reporting, prompt remedial acts and significant cooperation with the SEC's investigation.

- **Johnson & Johnson** – The company paid US$70 million dollars in 2011 to settle criminal and civil FCPA charges for bribes to public sector doctors in Greece. Its subsidiary DePuy Inc. was charged in a criminal complaint with conspiracy and violations of the FCPA. A former DePuy executive in the U.K., Robert John Dougall, was jailed for a year after he pleaded guilty in a London court to making £4.5 million pounds (US$7.36 million dollars) in corrupt payments to Greek medical professionals[67].

Recent FCPA cases such as those mentioned above highlight several themes:

- **SEC Reliance on Administrative Actions** - The SEC is increasingly relying on administrative actions to enforce FCPA violations, due to the increased authority it has been given under the 2010 Dodd-Frank Wall Street Reform and Consumer Protection Act amendments to the Securities and Exchange Act of 1934, as amended. Such amendments enable the SEC to pursue civil penalties through administrative

---

[66] SEC Charges Goodyear with FCPA Violations, February 24, 2015 at http://www.sec.gov/news/pressrelease/2015-38.html.
[67] Ibidem.

proceedings. In 2014, all eight SEC enforcement actions were resolved using the SEC's administrative process rather than through the use of a civil complaint.

- **DOJ Focus on Corporate Executives** - It is not only companies, which are the current target for FCPA prosecution and enforcement. The DOJ has been aggressively prosecuting corporate executives, both U.S. and foreign residents alike, who conspire to violate the FCPA. Therefore, individual responsibility for FCPA violations is becoming more widespread.

- **The DOJ's Role as Quasi-Enforcer** - The DOJ continues to act as a quasi-regulator by imposing reforms, compliance controls and behavioral changes with regard to FCPA enforcement. It has done so via plea agreements, deferred prosecution agreements ("DPAs") or non-prosecution agreements ("NPAs"). There is a trend, however, towards bringing more and bigger cases under the FCPA and reduced use of DPAs.

- **Both the DOJ and SEC are Encouraging Self-Disclosure and Cooperation** - The DOJ and SEC continue to give meaningful credit to corporations who cooperate with regard to FCPA infractions. In January 2015, the SEC announced a deferred prosecution agreement with PBSJ Corporation.[68] The DPA defers SEC charges for a period of two years and requires the company to comply with certain undertakings, in addition to US$3.4 million in financial remedies. This agreement shows the SEC's willingness to offer a significantly reduced penalty due to PBSJ Corporation's actions in quickly ending the misconduct after self-reporting to the SEC, voluntarily making witnesses available for interviews, and providing factual chronologies, timelines, internal summaries and full forensic images to cooperate with the SEC's investigation. In February 2015, at the PLI SEC Speaks session in Washington,

---

[68] SEC Charges Former Executive of Tampa-Based Engineering Firm with FCPA Violations, January 22, 2015 at http://www.sec.gov/news/pressrelease/2015-13.html#.VOzyZ1Uo5ow.

DC, Ms. Kara N. Brockmeyer (Chief of the FCPA Unit) outlined the following means by which a company may obtain credit for cooperation with the SEC:

- Real-time reporting of the company's investigation and findings, allowing the SEC to leverage these findings into its own investigation and interview witnesses contemporaneously;
- Translating witness interviews into English;
- Bringing foreign employees to the U.S. for interviews;
- When the wrongdoer is or was an employee, letting the SEC know that the employee has already left or will be terminated;
- Helping the SEC interview witnesses; and
- Thinking creatively to provide the necessary documentation to the SEC rather than using foreign data protection laws to block their production.

The FCPA also requires companies whose securities are listed in the U.S. to meet its accounting provisions[69]. These accounting provisions, which were designed to operate in tandem with the anti-bribery provisions of the FCPA, require corporations covered by the provisions to make and keep books and records that accurately and fairly reflect the transactions of the corporation and to devise and maintain an adequate system of internal accounting controls. An increasing number of corporations are taking additional steps to protect their reputation and reducing exposure by employing the services of due diligence companies. Identifying government-owned companies in an effort to identify easily overlooked government officials is rapidly becoming a critical component of more advanced anti-corruption programs.

Regarding payments to foreign officials, the act draws a distinction between bribery and facilitation or *grease payments*, which may be permissible under the FCPA but may still violate local laws. The primary distinction is that grease payments are made to an

[69] See FCPA Act See 15 U.S.C. § 78m.

official to expedite his performance of the duties he is already bound to perform. Payments to foreign officials may be legal under the FCPA if the payments are permitted under the written laws of the host country. Certain payments or reimbursements relating to product promotion may also be permitted under the FCPA.

In addition, the Travel Act, enacted into law in 1961, forbids the use of travel and communications means to commit state or federal crimes. Mostly, it's been used to prosecute domestic crimes, such as the Racketeer Influenced and Corrupt Organizations Act[70] (RICO) and gambling violations committed either by individuals or groups of persons.

Whistleblowing

On July 21, 2010, President Obama signed into law the Dodd-Frank Wall Street Reform and Consumer Protection Act (Dodd-Frank Act) and its sweeping financial regulatory reforms. Included among the provisions is a new whistleblower program which provides substantial cash rewards for whistleblowers who voluntarily provide information to the SEC leading to the successful prosecution of securities law violations.

Under the Dodd-Frank Act, a whistleblower is defined as a person who provides information relating to a violation of the securities laws to the SEC and the anti-retaliation provisions kick in when a person is penalized for blowing the whistle. Whistleblowers who report securities violations, including violations of the FCPA, that result in monetary sanctions greater than $1 million, may receive between 10 and 30 percent of the total recovery. The record penalties reported in several recent FCPA matters create significant financial incentives to report violations. In this year alone, there have been

---

[70] Commonly referred to as the RICO Act, this is a U.S. federal law that provides for extended criminal penalties and a civil cause of action for acts performed as part of an ongoing criminal organization. The RICO Act focuses specifically on racketeering, and it allows the leaders of a syndicate to be tried for the crimes which they ordered others to do or assisted them, closing a perceived loophole that allowed someone who told a man to, for example, murder, to be exempt from the trial because he did not actually commit the crime personally.

three settlements of FCPA-related matters exceeding $300 million each.[71]

Through their knowledge of the circumstances and individuals involved, whistleblowers can help SEC and DOJ identify potential violations much earlier than might otherwise have been possible, thus allowing SEC and DOJ to minimize the harm to investors, better preserve the integrity of the U.S. capital markets, and more swiftly hold accountable those responsible for unlawful conduct.

Recent changes to the U.S. FCPA introduced by the Sarbanes-Oxley Act of 2002 and the Dodd-Frank Act of 2010, which both contain provisions affecting whistleblowers who report FCPA violations, now allows and relies on whistleblowers as Sarbanes-Oxley prohibits issuers from retaliating against whistleblowers. It also provides that employees who are retaliated against for reporting possible securities law violations may file a complaint with the Department of Labor, for which they would be eligible to receive reinstatement, back pay, and other compensation.[72] Sarbanes-Oxley also prohibits retaliation against employee whistleblowers under the obstruction of justice statute.

Therefore, individuals can report possible securities law violations on any U.S. company, or any company traded on U.S. exchanges, and potentially collect millions of dollars. If a person knows of any improper payments, offers, or gifts made by a company to obtain an advantage in a business in the U.S. or abroad they are encouraged to report it. There are several law firms in the U.S. set up to assist whistleblowers in reporting their suspicions.

---

[71] BAE Systems plc's Plea Agreement with the Department of Justice dated February 4, 2010; Snamprogetti Netherland B.V.'s Deferred Prosecution Agreement with the Department of Justice dated July 7, 2010; Final Judgment as to Snamprogetti Netherlands B.V. entered in the action of SEC v. ENI, S.p.A, Civil Action No.: 4:10-cv-02414 on July 7, 2010; Final Judgment as to ENI, S.p.A entered in the action of SEC v. ENI, S.p.A, Civil Action No.: 4:10-cv-02414 on July 7, 2010; Technip S.A.'s Deferred Prosecution Agreement with the Department of Justice dated June 28, 2010; Final Judgment as to Technip S.A. entered in the action of SEC v. Technip S.A., Civil Action No.: 4:10-cv-02289 on June 28, 2010.

[72] 18 U.S.C. § 1513(e).

There is no materiality to this act, making it illegal to offer anything of value as a bribe, including cash or non-cash items. The government focuses on the intent of the bribery rather than on the amount.

Consequently, companies operating overseas should take immediate action to prepare for additional scrutiny and disclosure risks posed by the whistleblower provision. Maintaining regular and recurrent training and developing effective compliance programs are as important as ever. Legal and compliance professionals are well advised to reevaluate their internal controls designed to detect improper payments, internal audit programs, and the procedures by which employees can report questionable conduct to in-house compliance personnel. Companies with known violations or ongoing internal investigations also face new challenges evaluating whether and when to voluntarily self-report violations to the SEC and DOJ.

Potential whistleblower disclosures to the SEC pose a particular and significant impact on companies subject to the FCPA given the sustained regulatory focus on anti-corruption compliance and controls, the pressure to self-report potential violations to government authorities, and the dramatic increase in the number of prosecutions.

The Whistleblower Provision

Codified as Section 21F of the Securities Exchange Act of 1934, the whistleblower provision provides for the SEC to reward individuals who voluntarily report independently derived information leading to the successful prosecution of securities law violations if monetary recoveries exceed $1 million.[73] To be eligible for an award, the whistleblower must provide the SEC with "original information."[74] By original information SEC means that:

---

[73] Dodd-Frank Wall Street Reform and Consumer Protection Act, H.R. 4173, 111th Cong. § 922a(b)(1) (2010) [hereinafter "Dodd-Frank Act"].
[74] Dodd-Frank Act § 922a(b)(1).

1. It must be "derived from the independent knowledge or analysis of the whistleblower"
2. It cannot be known to the SEC from any other source; and
3. It cannot be "exclusively derived from an allegation made in a judicial or administrative hearing, in a governmental report, hearing, audit, or investigation, or from the news media."[75]

While "bits and pieces" of the whistleblower's information may be derived or previously known to the media, the whistleblower must provide critical information that was unknown to the SEC and led to the success of the government's case. The SEC is permitted to share information derived from a whistleblower with other federal, state and foreign law enforcement authorities.

Becoming a FCPA whistleblower may entitle the individual to receive substantial compensation, potentially millions of dollars. New changes in U.S. laws now allow individuals reporting FCPA violations to receive full protection from retaliation and collect up to 30% of the fines that the government collects. The U.S. government can fine companies up to US$2 million dollars for each violation of the law. Thus for each payment made and for each false record there may be a fine levied even if the payments are small. In 2010 the U.S. government collected over $1.5 billion dollars in FCPA fines.

The SEC exercises discretion over the amount of the reward within a range of 10 to 30 percent of the aggregate amount recovered, including disgorgement, penalties, and interest. The amount recovered includes not only monies collected by the SEC, but also fines and penalties assessed by the DOJ, self- regulatory organizations, and state attorneys general. In setting the reward amount, the SEC is to consider three factors:

- The significance of the information provided to the success of the SEC's action

[75] Dodd-Frank Act § 922a(a)(3).

- The degree of assistance provided by the whistleblower and the whistleblower's representative in the SEC's action; and
- The SEC's interest in deterring securities law violations by rewarding whistleblowers.

The Dodd-Frank Act defines individuals who can qualify as whistleblowers broadly. For example, the law does not appear to require that the individual be a U.S. national, which opens the door for employees of foreign subsidiaries to seek whistleblower status. Certain individuals, however, are not eligible to collect an award, such as employees of the securities regulators and auditors. Most notably, individuals convicted of a criminal violation related to the SEC's enforcement action also are barred from receiving an award. Thus, whether an individual who is implicated in the underlying conduct can obtain a reward as a whistleblower will depend, in part, on whether he is ultimately convicted on related criminal charges.

The whistleblower provision also provides anti-retaliation protections, which permit civil causes of action for wrongful termination, suspension, harassment, or other discrimination because of the whistleblower's reporting to the SEC. If successful, an anti-retaliation claim can result in reinstatement of seniority, two times the amount of back pay otherwise owed with interest, and compensation for litigation costs, expert witness fees and reasonable attorney's fees.

This new whistleblower incentive greatly expands the SEC's previous insider trading bounty program, which applied solely to reporting of insider trading violations and civil penalties recovered, and did not provide guaranteed minimum rewards. Historically, the insider-trading program generated few enforcement actions or substantial rewards for whistleblowers.

However, on July 23, 2010, the SEC announced an award of $1 million to the ex-wife and current husband of a Microsoft employee for helping to reopen an insider trading case involving trading in Pequot Capital Management. This was by far the largest award the SEC had ever paid under the program. Authorities are hopeful that guaranteed awards to parties who provide information leading to recovery of penalties and disgorgement in a broader range of cases will yield greater reporting and prosecutions, as well as additional compliance measures to prevent such violations in the first instance.

Compliance and Internal Reporting

Given the nearly constant press reports of new FCPA prosecutions and staggering penalty amounts, the enactment of the whistleblower provision provides yet another reason for companies to assess and ensure the adequacy of their anti-corruption compliance programs. The effectiveness of internal controls, audit functions, and internal reporting procedures should be evaluated in light of these developments.

To reduce the risk of employees reporting merely suspicious activity to the SEC rather than through internal compliance procedures, companies should maintain effective internal reporting systems that offer employees an avenue by which to report their compliance concerns to compliance personnel. Employees should be properly trained on utilizing internal reporting procedures, and made confident that their concerns will be taken seriously and adequately investigated.

Further, companies with active and effective internal reporting programs are more likely to obtain information that may not be captured through existing internal controls or internal audit programs. While internal reporting procedures will not protect the company from employees who are motivated to provide information directly to the SEC rather than through corporate channels in hopes of cashing in on a reward, effective procedures may encourage employees that concerns can be adequately addressed through the company's compliance program.

Investigations and Self-Disclosure

The whistleblower provision also raises new issues for companies conducting internal investigations of potential securities law violations. Preferably, companies should be permitted to review and adequately investigate suspicious conduct before determining whether such conduct violates the securities laws and should be self-reported to government authorities. The strong incentives created by the Dodd-Frank Act for individual employees to be the first to report new information about potentially violating conduct to the SEC, however, creates added challenges to maintaining the confidentiality of an investigation.

Companies undertaking investigations must assess and continue to reassess the risks and benefits of self-reporting under the increased likelihood that an employee knowledgeable of the conduct or investigation may contact the SEC before the company self-reports. The DOJ and SEC consider self- disclosure when recommending leniency in penalties for FCPA violations and, in doing so, have encouraged companies to report known violations.

Note, however, that a company's self-reporting to the SEC may not foreclose a whistleblower from receiving an award for information provided after the company discloses to the SEC. In such a case, the relevant inquiry would be whether the whistleblower provided additional "original information" to the SEC that had not been disclosed by the company.

This suggests that companies that self-report need to carefully consider the sufficiency of information provided to regulators. Should the SEC staff determine that a company provided inaccurate or misleading information, it likely will seek harsh penalties from the company when making enforcement recommendations.

Finally, given the anti-retaliatory protections afforded to whistleblowers, special care should be taken while instructing employees to maintain the confidentiality of an investigation. It is important that confidentiality directives aimed to protect the integrity of the investigative process are not interpreted as efforts to prevent employees from contacting the SEC as a whistleblower.

Nonetheless, in 2014, in Liu v. Siemens AG, the Second Circuit limited the reach of the Act's anti-retaliation protections to domestic whistleblowers. In doing so, the Court rejected a claim brought by a Taiwanese lawyer employed by a German corporation who disclosed suspected Foreign Corrupt Practices Act violations by the corporation's Chinese subsidiary, finding that the relevant provisions of the Dodd-Frank Act did not apply "extraterritorially." Although the Court's decision is significant in its impact on foreign whistleblowers, leaving them vulnerable to employer retaliation and raising questions about what facts sufficiently may link the retaliation to the United States, it also is significant for the issues it does not address such as whether the Act's protections apply to employees who blow the whistle internally rather than to the SEC. Also, whether the statute applies to FCPA violations at all. The first issue intentionally was left unanswered by the Second Circuit. Many believed that the question of the Act's applicability to internal reports, which also was sidestepped by the district court in Liu, would be addressed by the Second Circuit because of current disagreement among federal courts on this point.

A number of federal district courts have found that the anti-retaliation provision of the Act is triggered where an employee makes an internal report of misconduct despite the statute's definition of whistleblower. Indeed, the SEC itself has assumed this position, filing an amicus brief in the Liu case urging the Second Circuit to give deference to the agency's rule granting protection from retaliation under Dodd-Frank to employees who make protected disclosures irrespective of whether they report the information to the SEC or another source.

Assistance and information from a whistleblower that knows of possible securities law violations can be among the most powerful weapons in the law enforcement arsenal of FCPA. Figure 4.5 provides contact information on SEC's office of the whistleblower.

SEC Office of the Whistleblower

100 F Street NE, Mail Stop 5971
Washington, DC 20549
Facsimile: (703) 813-9322
Online Report Form: http://www.sec.gov/whistleblower

Figure 4.5 – SEC office of the whistleblower.

Chapter 5 - FCPA Criticism

Overview

Ideally, the FCPA not only prevents engagement in corruption, but also causes other nations to limit bribery as an incentive for US investment. However, the FCPA fails because it is vague, injurious and ultimately overreaching. Instead, the US would benefit from adhering to a strict domestic anti-bribery policy, encouraging similar policies abroad and imposing trade sanctions against countries engaging in bribery.

Bribery is generally accepted as a harmful practice as it subverts the natural order of the free marketplace, harms economic growth, misdirects investment, thereby wasting resources, and breeds distrust in the government. The FCPA attempts to counter these effects by, first, prohibiting all bribes made by U.S. firms to foreign officials and, second, requiring strict record-keeping procedures of all monetary transactions abroad. There is some flexibility in the form of "grease payments" for "routine governmental actions," which mainly include payments to expedite legal government actions.

Main FCPA Criticisms

While the FCPA has the unquestionably noble goal of eliminating corruption and holding the U.S. concerns to a high standard of morality, it has come under recent criticism for the substantial and, some would say, anti-competitive, costs that it imposes. Criticism of the FCPA includes the policy's ambiguity and its negative repercussions for American companies. This chapter tries to address the most important ones.

Most ambiguity in the FCPA concerns the requirements on what factors make payments illegal. Uncertainties include:

- Who qualifies as a foreign official? The line between public officials and those of private companies is often unclear. For instance, in China, many private businesspeople qualify as foreign officials because their companies are partially state-owned-enterprises, and payments to these companies are subject to scrutiny.
- What qualifies as "grease payments"? These differ from bribery in the purpose of the payment, not the duties of the recipient. If the payment is without a corrupt motive, then it isn't bribery. Intent, however, is hard to determine in court; thus, US firms avoid these payments even if they are legal.
- When is a parent corporation liable for its subsidiary's violation? Even domestic companies may be responsible for their international subsidiary's actions, and must spend time and money monitoring their foreign firms or choose not to have them at all.

The FCPA stipulations are lengthy, and unfortunately, in most cases, firms would rather not defend what might be legitimate and prohibit all foreign payments instead. However, this cripples American investment by limiting the types of business ventures with which companies are willing to become involved.

Another large criticism of the FCPA is its significant consequences for firms abroad. Reportedly, U.S. foreign direct investments (FDI) decreased 12 percent since FCPA was implemented. Furthermore, U.S. firms have lost many multi-million dollar opportunities by not paying the necessary people, as well as wasting time and resources tied up in FCPA investigations.

For example, in 2004, Lockheed Martin was forced to drop a $2.2 billion offer for Titan Corporation after Titan failed to resolve Department of Justice investigations of FCPA violations. Titan not only sacrificed the deal, but also had to pay $28.5 million in the settlement and Lockheed Martin lost out on a large acquisition. There are currently 104 firms under investigation for 2014, including big multi-national companies such as Citigroup, FedEx, Microsoft and Tesco.

Another repercussion is that American investment suffers in countries where expensive gifts and payments may not only be normal, but also courteous. In many Asian countries, for example, it is a common practice to give substantial gifts to ensure cooperation in business agreements.

The FCPA fails to accomplish its goals; however, minimizing American corruption is a justifiable aim. The only way to do this without crippling business ventures is to focus on strict domestic anti-bribery policy. By setting an example and helping others assess the damages of corruption and create and adhere to their own policies, the US could successfully navigate all of the listed shortcomings of the FCPA.

Another legitimate option would be to let market mechanisms inhibit corruption. The U.S. could impose trade sanctions such as tariffs and quotas against foreign bribers, and provide contract terms in settlements prohibiting paying and accepting bribes. Similarly, people's taste could help curb bribery. If all payment records enforced by the FCPA were made public knowledge, then the reputations and standings of both the companies and governments involved in bribery would be affected accordingly.

In December 2011, the New York City Bar Association's Committee on International Business Transactions issued a report critical of the FCPA, and, perhaps more significantly, its enforcement.[76]

The report noted that the FCPA imposes substantial compliance costs on companies subject to its jurisdiction — costs that their foreign competitors may not face. It also lamented the seemingly unchecked prosecutorial power to obtain huge settlements in FCPA cases, as the consequences of an FCPA indictment are potentially fatal to a company, and, as a result, most companies are willing to settle for large sums — regardless of whether they believe the allegations are valid. Indeed, as the report notes, in April 2011, each of the eight top fines for FCPA "violations" exceeded $100 million.

The report expressed the concern that the U.S. DOJ is both prosecutor and judge in the FCPA context and that some U.S. companies have ceased foreign operations in the face of the uncertainty of FCPA enforcement. To that end, the report makes a number of recommendations to reign in the FCPA, such as adding a "willfulness" requirement before imposing liability on corporations, which can currently be criminally liable without having knowledge of the wrongful conduct, to ensure that only those companies that intend to violate the law are subject to the harsh fines, as well as a provision limiting a company's successor liability for the premerger FCPA violations of a company that it acquired.

In an article titled *State Hypocrisy on Anti-Bribery Laws*, Stephan Kinsella[77] argues that the duplicity of

---

[76] "The FCPA and its Impact on International Business Transactions — Should Anything be Done to Minimize the Consequences of the U.S.'s Unique Position on Combating Offshore Corruption?", New York City Bar Association, (Dec. 2011), http://www2.nycbar.org/pdf/report/uploads/FCPAImpactonInternationalBusinessTransactions.pdf. Last accessed on 12/18/2013.

[77] Kinsella is an American intellectual property lawyer and libertarian legal theorist. His legal works have been published by Oceana Publications, which was acquired in 2005 by Oxford University Press and West/Thomson Reuters.

"FCPA is blinding, as it makes it okay for the state to bribe (and extort and coerce) private business by means of threats, subsidies, tax breaks, and protectionist legislation, and okay for businesses to bribe elected officials (campaign contributions), and okay for the U.S. administration to bribe foreign governments, and okay for U.S. companies to be forced to pay bribes in the form of taxes, that are less than the amount of bribes they would have to pay to foreign officials, but not okay for U.S. companies to bribe foreign officials–even if this is customary and essential to "doing business" in that country, despite the fact this puts American businesses at a competitive disadvantage with companies from other countries that do not prohibit such bribery."

As Lew Rockwell,[78] former congressional chief of staff to U.S. senator Ron Paul, noted in his article *Extortion, Private and Public: The Case of Chiquita Banana,*[79]

"Paying bribes and being subject to this kind of extortion is just part of what it takes to do business in many countries. This might sound awful, but the truth is that such payments are often less than the companies would be paying to the tax man in the U.S., which runs a similar kind of extortion scam but with legal cover."[80]

In Rockwell's opinion, American businesses are howling at the competitive disadvantage this Act imposes on them. Instead of repealing this FCPA Act, Rockwell argues the U.S. is using its legislative imperialism to force other countries to adopt similar laws, while twisting the arms of other countries in a number of areas,

[78] Mr. Rockwell was also the former editorial assistant to Ludwig von Mises institute. He is the founder and chairman of the Mises Institute, and the executor for the estate of Murray N. Rothbard, and editor of LewRockwell.com.
[79] http://archive.lewrockwell.com/rockwell/case-of-chiquita-banana185.html, last accessed on 12/14/2013.
[80] Ibidem.

including intellectual property, antitrust law, central banking policies, oil & gas ownership by the state, environmental standards, labor standards, tax levels and policy, and so on. It did this mainly by pushing the OECD Anti-Bribery Convention, now ratified by 38 states, which are required by the Convention to implement FCPA style laws nationally. The UK has just done so in The UK Bribery Act.[81]

It is important to note that the FCPA does not contain a private right of action. Hence, only the government can enforce the Act. But, private complainants have steadily found creative ways to use FCPA violations as predicate acts in private causes of action. These private actions are often opportunistic in that they are usually commenced after a government investigation has become public, and they use admissions and settlements in the government context to further their own causes of action.

For example, in 2010, Innospec Inc. pleaded guilty to violating the FCPA by bribing officials in Iraq and Indonesia to ensure sales of its product in those areas. It agreed to pay $14.1 million dollars in penalties and to retain an independent compliance monitor for three years to oversee the imposition of an anti-corruption compliance protocol. On the same day, it also settled a civil complaint with the U.S. SEC, requiring it to disgorge $11.2 million dollars in profits.[82]

After Innospec plead guilty, its competitor, NewMarket Corp., brought claims against it for antitrust violations[83]. NewMarket claimed that Innospec paid bribes to the Iraqi and Indonesian governments so that those governments would favor Innospec's product, would not transition to NewMarket's product, and would

[81] http://www.legislation.gov.uk/ukpga/2010/23/contents.

[82] Press Release, Department of Justice, Innospec Inc. Pleads Guilty to FCPA Charges and Defrauding United Nations; Admits to Violating the U.S. Embargo Against Cuba (March 18, 2010), http://www.justice.gov/opa/pr/2010/March/10-crm-278.html. Last accessed on 12/10/2013.

[83] Second Amended Complaint ¶ 1, Newmarket Corp. v. Innospec Inc., No. 3:10-cv-00503 (E.D.Va. Jan. 27, 2011) (ECF No. 41).

therefore maintain Innospec's monopoly in those markets. Pointedly, NewMarket's principal financial officer, David Fiorenza, said that it was only after reading about the plea that he learned about Innospec's actions,[84] which would eventually form the basis of NewMarket's complaint. This case ultimately settled in October 2011 when Innospec agreed to pay NewMarket $45 million dollars.[85]

The lack of a compliance defense, as shown in Innospec's case, is particularly problematic in the successor liability context, as a company does not have a defense under the FCPA for the corrupt actions of an acquired company, even if the acquiring company adhered to its compliance program by conducting a rigorous due diligence investigation, although ultimately failing to uncover the corrupt acts.

In light of the government's resistance to efforts to amend the FCPA and the pace of recent FCPA enforcement, the addition of a corporate willfulness requirement or a compliance program defense is unlikely in the short term. Nor can one expect to see the elimination of successor liability. With this legal environment, companies should focus on effectively implementing a compliance program, while actively looking for opportunities to ensure that other companies, particularly competitors, are not able to reap the benefits of illegal acts.

Ultimately, although the FCPA's attempt to reduce corruption is well intentioned, it has only harmed economic interests abroad due to its ambiguity and restrictiveness. A more fruitful policy would maintain a hard domestic anti-bribery policy, encourage contracts prohibiting bribes and let the social standing of corrupt firms suffer. This way, the U.S. can stay true to its tradition of

[84] Emily C. Dooley, Richmond firm claims in suit that competitor paid kickbacks to Iraqis, Richmond Times- Dispatch (Aug. 5, 2010), at B-03.

[85] Bruce Carton, Company Allegedly Bumped Out of Contract by Rival's Corruption Recovers $45 Million in Civil Settlement, Compliance Week, (Oct. 5, 2011), http://www.complianceweek.com/company-allegedly-   bumped-out-of-contract-by-rivalscorruption- recovers-45-million-in-civil-settlement/article/213666/. Last accessed on 12/10/2013.

freedom in the marketplace while allowing firms to grow and invest where they need.

Chapter 6 - Preventing Corruption and FCPA Violations

Overview

With the rapid development of the Web, cross border investigative process is literally assaulted and overwhelmed by huge quantities of data. To process and understand these data, due diligence personnel, and investigators, must make use of software and Web tools. To chart up and track down potential criminal enterprises, one can use software applications such as Mindjet[86] or IBM's I2.[87]

Web Tools

While Mindjet is more generic software for brainstorming data, I2 provides intelligence analysis, law enforcement and fraud

---

[86] www.mindjet.com.

[87] http://www-01.ibm.com/software/info/i2software/

investigation solutions, delivering flexible capabilities that help combat crime, terrorism and fraudulent activity. Jay Liebowitz's book on information analysis, *Strategic Intelligence: Business Intelligence, Competitive Intelligence, and Knowledge Management*[88], describes I2's use in cases of major investigations on prescription-drug-diversion fraud and other scenarios. I2, Pajek,[89] UCInet[90] and similar software are ultimate tools for cross-border investigative tasks and will provide new value to due diligence process when trading abroad.

European Business Registry

The European Business Registry (EBR) database[91] is another very efficient tool for due diligence process in an attempt to prevent an investor in dealing with a corrupt organization abroad. The database, depicted in Figure 6.1, has unified data contained in registries of commerce in Austria, Belgium, Denmark, Estonia, Finland, France, Germany, Greece, Ireland, Italy, Jersey, Latvia, Netherlands, Norway, Serbia, Spain, Sweden, Ukraine, and UK. Name-based searches are possible. Prices differ from country to country and are mentioned with each search.

---

[88] Auerbach Publications, 2006.

[89] Pajek, a Slovene word for Spider, is a program for analysis and visualization of large networks. It is freely available, for noncommercial use, at its download page at http://pajek.imfm.si/doku.php?id=download.

[90] UCINET is a software for analyzing social network data.

[91] http://www.ebr.org

Figure 6.1 - The European Business Registry database unifies registries of commerce from several European countries. SOURCE: EBR

Lexis-Nexis

Another excellent software application is Lexis-Nexis,[92] as depicted in Figure 6.2. It requires subscription and payment. Lexis-Nexis is a gathering of databases and it offers access to media reports, company registrars in many countries, court cases, financial markets information, people's searches and many others. One useful tool inside Lexis-Nexis is access to the Dun & Bradstreet companies database, which covers the whole world. Usually companies involved in imports-exports are listed in this database.

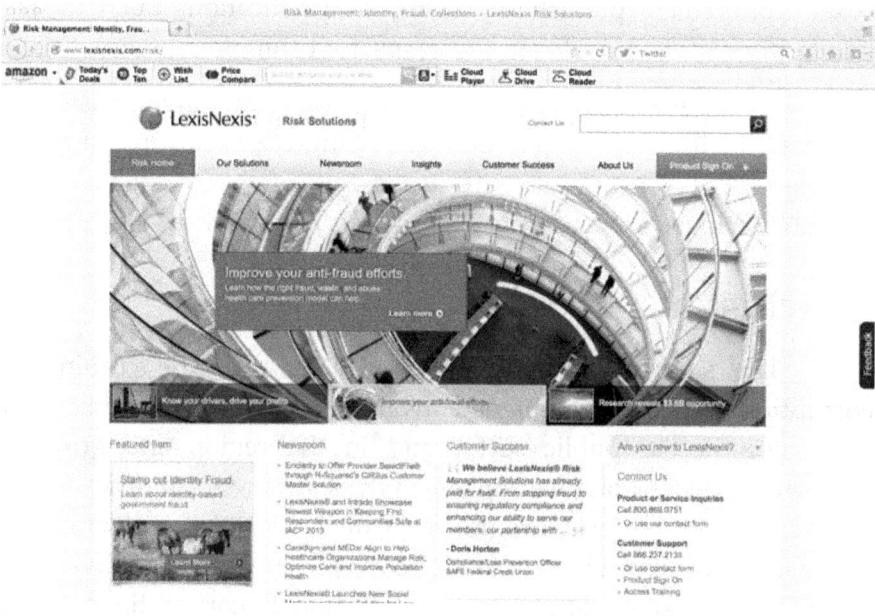

Figure 6.2 – The LexisNexis database offers access to media reports, company registrars in many countries, court cases, financial markets information, people's searches and many others.

[92] http://www.lexisnexis.com/risk/

National Association of Secretaries of State

The U.S. has a wealth of databases, which can be used in order to track down suspicious corporations. A useful web portal towards these databases is the National Association of Secretaries of State (NASS) at http://www.nass.org. You will need to register with the portal, free of charge, in order to then have access to the registrar of companies of 50 states plus the District of Columbia.

Global Legal Information Network

Another very good resource is the Global Legal Information Network (GLIN), at http://www.glin.gov, which is a public database of laws, regulations, judicial decisions, and other complementary legal sources contributed by governmental agencies and international organizations. You can find in it data on Paraguay based companies, published on official publications such as the *Gaceta Oficial de la Republica del Paraguay*, for example.

There are many other resources to assist any investor or organization in conducting a sound due diligence regarding a foreign company. These listed here are just a few of the many resources available, which escape the objective of this book and chapter.

Conclusion

The support of international agencies for the curbing of corruption indicates heightened awareness about the problem of corruption in the public sector and in the region and growing concern on the part of governments in these different countries to put in place structures and programs to deal with the problem. The increasing concern about the dangers of corruption among the emerging markets, often by multinational corporations from advanced economies, and the need for urgent action needs to be matched by a similar sense of urgency in the G7 and G20 summits. In the final analysis, the political will to empower and support those whose task it is to discover, investigate, reveal, and punish corruption in the public sector will be the major determinant of success. Support from these summits could assist in that regard.

In our opinion, the international business community should work more closely with law enforcement to detect patterns and methods of organized crime, since so many crimes fund terrorism. More detailed analysis of the operation of illicit activities around the world would help advance an understanding of wide spread corruption, crime and terrorist financing. Corruption overseas, which is so often linked to facilitating organized crime and terrorism, should be elevated to a U.S. national security concern with an operational focus. A joint task force composed of analysts from the Federal Bureau of Investigation (FBI), Department of Homeland Security (DHS) and the Central Intelligence Agency (CIA), as well as the Interpol, should be formed to create an integrated system for data collection and analysis. A broader view of today's terrorist and criminal groups is needed, given that their methods and their motives are often shared.

Chapter 7 - FCPA Effects on Foreign Investments

Overview

An ongoing debate, however, asks about the law's effects. Recent research has found evidence that the FCPA discourages foreign investment.[93] Companies engaging in merging and acquisition (M&A) in emerging and frontier markets face a uniquely increased level of regulatory and corruption risk.[94]

When looking at the outcome of the law, however, it appears to have a positive effect. The growth of American multinational corporations (MNC's) in the last few years confirms that briberies are not basic facts of businesses in many countries, but it doesn't mean that bribery doesn't exist. Even though government and companies have taken important steps, much more needs to be done because bribery continues to be a problem in many countries.

[93] Graham, Bradley, Stroup, Caleb (2016). "Does Anti-bribery Enforcement Deter Foreign Investment?" (PDF). Applied Economics Letters. doi:10.1080/13504851.2015.1049333.

[94] Brooks, Robin; Stacey, Oliver; Jarman, Daniel. "Tackling Corruption and Regulatory Risk in M&A Transactions". Transaction Advisors. ISSN 2329-9134.

Impact on FDI

The severity of criminal and civil penalties ordered in recent FCPA cases has received widespread notoriety and encouraged prudent corporations to exercise extreme caution when dealing with foreign corporations and governments. The overemphasis on policing corruption abroad, and the extraterritorial application of criminal sanctions to enforce U.S. cultural prejudices, places U.S. companies at a substantial competitive disadvantage when seeking business relationships in countries where the culture permits the kind of practices that the FCPA prohibits. Moreover, the rise of China as both an importer and an exporter of foreign direct investment (FDI) pose a serious challenge to the efficacy of the FCPA as a deterrent to corruption.[95]

Historically a nation wary of FDI, China has embraced in the past twenty years a modern, market-oriented system that caters heavily to international business. Such change does not come without its share of challenges. China embraces deep-rooted traditions, some of which test the boundaries of the Western world's moral and ethical principles. Bribery, as understood under the FCPA, is a perfect example; it is not just common, but runs rampant throughout China's business practices and is accepted as a valid means of doing business.

China's economic ascendance and its cultural acceptance of bribery challenge the prevailing U.S. anti-corruption legal regime in two ways. First, U.S. companies operating in China encounter an ethics and compliance minefield, with bribery and corruption impeding successful business operations. Western companies that want to compete in China's booming market must understand the unique cultural and legal processes that shape business transactions in the country, while at the same time not running afoul of U.S. law. Second, Chinese companies now compete with U.S. companies for investment opportunities in emerging economies. Chinese companies

---

[95] See Michael B. Bixby, The Lion Awakens: The Foreign Corrupt Practices Act—1977 to 2010, 12 SAN DIEGO INT'L L.J. 89, 115–18 (2010).

are not generally subject to strictly enforced anti-bribery legislation such as the FCPA, and the absence of any such regulation gives Chinese companies a competitive advantage over U.S. companies in the global marketplace by allowing them to curry favor with local officials in ways that U.S. companies cannot.

Moreover, the increasing globalization of business, exemplified by China's rise as both an importer and exporter of FDI, is generating a corresponding globalization of law enforcement efforts, which one can see in the increasingly prominent enforcement of the FCPA. Although the frequency of FCPA enforcement has risen sharply, it has yet to produce a commensurate rise in legal scholarship considering its effect on U.S. outbound FDI opportunities. While scholars in the last three decades surveyed issues concerning the moral and economic rationales for the FCPA, with frequent concern given to the problems created by cultural relativism, they have yet to engage in the more fundamental question of whether the statute's impact mirrors its original purpose.

Although the purpose of the FCPA is to deter bribery in a manner that aids the United States in building international economic and political alliances, the latest empirical studies reveal that the dogmatic application of the law has contributed to an erosion of the position of U.S. companies in certain countries. In countries where bribery is considered relatively common, the FCPA's current enforcement scheme is ineffective, if not counterproductive, in preventing corruption.

U.S. companies subject to the FCPA are hard-pressed to compete in those countries and in some cases may be deterred from even trying. Companies based in countries not subject to strictly enforced anti- bribery legislation, such as China, have taken advantage of the unleveled playing field, and corruption continues unabated. This dynamic creates myriad ethical, economic, and foreign policy problems for the United States, which are particularly manifest in China's aggressive investment in the emerging economies of countries commonly perceived in the United States to tolerate corruption, such Angola, Sudan, the Democratic Republic of

Congo, and other African countries. By enforcing the FCPA without regard to its collateral effects, the United States unwittingly sacrifices both poverty reduction and outbound FDI opportunities in order to combat bribery both in China and other emerging economies.

While deterring bribery is certainly a worthy goal, it is far wiser to deter bribery as part of an ongoing business relationship rather than as a prerequisite to conducting business. Indeed, incentivizing ethical business in emerging markets is precisely the goal of the FCPA. The challenge of China as both an importer and exporter of FDI should encourage U.S. policymakers to revisit the text and enforcement scheme of the FCPA so that the law will be more effective in curbing nefarious business practices without placing U.S. companies at a severe competitive disadvantage.

Impact on International Business

As an international business consultant and research of the discipline, focusing on international management, cross-border mergers and acquisitions and other international affairs, I have witnessed a significant increase in the effects of the FCPA in the past decade. A large portion of my consulting engagements is devoted to training and advising on FCPA compliancy to U.S. corporations operating abroad ad well as foreign corporations traded in the U.S. or staffed with U.S. nationals. Overall, companies that are subject to the FCPA—including all U.S. companies and non-U.S. companies that have equity securities listed on a U.S. exchange—have become increasingly wary of purchasing businesses that have not operated under the Act for fear of acquiring very costly liabilities. I assist companies in this process and have devised an extensive due diligence process that should be followed, partnering with law firms and CPAs to augment the process along the way. The reality is that most companies are discouraged to invest abroad due to the expensive time and complexity of the process.

Similarly, companies that are not subject to the FCPA express substantial reservations about engaging in transactions that would bring them under the Act's jurisdiction, including listing their equity securities on a U.S. exchange through an IPO or capital raising transaction--choosing instead to list it in other foreign exchange in Europe or Asia-- or by acquiring a U.S. company in a stock-for-stock merger or exchange offer.

The effects of the FCPA on transactions are manifested mainly in four areas:

- Transaction costs, such as the increased due diligence efforts I cited above,
- Post-transaction integration costs, such as adding appropriate FCPA compliance procedures to an acquired company or across a company that was not previously subject to the FCPA
- The increased risk of exposure to an enforcement action and related costs, such as internal investigations and fines, and
- As a result of the foregoing and other effects of the FCPA, the non-pursuit or abandonment of transactions that otherwise would have been completed.

These FCPA-driven costs and considerations put companies covered by the FCPA, mostly U.S. companies and large, mature European companies, in a distinctively different regulatory position as compared to their non-covered competitors. In my experience, and in particular, recently, this asymmetry in regulation has had significant direct and indirect effects on companies subject to the FCPA as well as knock-on effects on the U.S. markets more generally.

The approach of the DOJ and SEC with regard to FCPA enforcement imposes a host of costs on companies subject to the Act. In addition to the more obvious costs of ensuring compliance, including the costs of due diligence, maintaining compliance programs and conducting internal investigations in the event indicia of corruption are present, companies face the more subtle costs of having to overcome other burdens that their competitors do not face, such as requiring foreign joint venture partners to adopt costly compliance measures and bear the risk of FCPA enforcement actions, and forgoing some overseas business opportunities altogether, such as in jurisdictions where the risk of corruption is so high that compliance efforts, no matter how costly, would not sufficiently reduce enforcement risk.

Non-U.S. Approaches To Combating International Corruption

There have been some noteworthy developments in the approaches of other countries to combating international corruption over the past 15 years. In 1997, the United States' efforts to create an international anti-corruption regime culminated with the adoption of the OECD Anti-Bribery Convention.[96] Among other things, Convention signatories are required to:

1. Criminalize bribery of foreign public officials
2. Hold corporations and other legal persons liable for bribery
3. Prohibit "off-the-books" payments and other accounting practices that may facilitate corruption
4. Make bribery an extraditable offense and
5. Provide mutual legal assistance to each other in bribery cases.[97]

The Convention does not include a specific set of legal rules that are required to be adopted. Instead, adoption of the Convention's principles is to be undertaken and evaluated on a "functional equivalence" basis, allowing different countries to use different methods, according to the idiosyncrasies of their individual legal systems.

[96] See Indira Carr & Opi Outhwaite, The OECD Anti-Bribery Convention Ten Years On, 5 MANCHESTER J. INT'L ECON. L. 3, 6 – 7 (2008). The Convention has been adopted by over 30 countries, and its standards were incorporated into the FCPA by the International Anti-Bribery and Fair Competition Act of 1998.

[97] Ibidem, p. 7–8.

The language and objectives of the Convention are very similar to the FCPA, which could suggest that participating countries have taken an approach to international corruption that is substantially similar to that of the United States. The data does not support this conclusion. While all state parties to the Convention have passed laws criminalizing foreign bribery, not all of these laws are effective in practice. For example, while the U.S. brought 67 prosecutions under the FCPA in 2006 – 2007, 15 countries, "including Australia, Mexico, New Zealand, and Portugal," brought none. Canada and Japan each brought only one prosecution, with relatively minor consequences.[98]

According to one report, from 2000 to 2010 U.S. authorities brought more than 3.5 times more foreign bribery enforcement actions than all other countries combined. These numbers are not proportionate to the level of international activity of each country and it is unlikely that these countries' corporations conduct international business substantially differently from those subject to the FCPA, and there are many companies that are subject to multiple regimes. While the UK recently increased its enforcement profile with the passage of the Bribery Act, it is only one country among the many signatories of the Convention.

Note that observers have cited a recent uptick in enforcement activities and fines by certain non-U.S. authorities as evidence of convergence among some Organization for Economic Co-operation and Development (OECD) countries. While this may be the case, however, this data also can be interpreted as demonstrating a "piggyback" phenomenon in certain jurisdictions, where there is a U.S. FCPA investigation or enforcement action, there is likely to be a parallel investigation and action, as well as additional costs imposed, by a non-U.S. authority. If this "piggybacking" is the reality in such jurisdictions, there is a widening, not a narrowing, of the gap between the burdens imposed on companies subject to the FCPA and

---

[98] See John Hatchard, Recent Developments in Combating the Bribery of Foreign Public Officials: A Cause for Optimism? 85 U. DET. MERCY L. REV. 1, 8 (2007).

those that are not. In other words, in some jurisdictions, companies subject to the FCPA are now at risk of being hit twice.

Strategically speaking, it is important to recognize that many countries that house important multinational enterprises (MNEs) are not parties to the OECD Convention.[99] It is incontrovertible that the economic activity in and involving these countries is increasing relative to both the United States and the other countries that are parties to the Convention and that the effectiveness of any transnational anti-corruption effort that does not cover these enterprises will necessarily be limited. A comparison that would provide valuable information but is difficult to make, partially because there are so few identifiable actions) is how many non-U.S. companies that are not subject to the FCPA have been subject to large fines or other sanctions for engaging in, or allegedly engaging in, foreign corruption.

We have therefore, although via a very simplistic statement, a global anti-corruption landscape that can be viewed as having three tiers: the FCPA, with expansive law and zealous enforcement; the other OECD Convention signatories, with law seemingly similar to the FCPA but lighter or with episodic enforcement; and a non-OECD signatories, with limited law and limited to no notable enforcement. The international business playing field is far from level, and American MNEs are at huge disadvantage.

The moral sense of the United States to "do the right thing" is clearly and laudably a motivating factor, and a noble one I must say and agree. The legislative history of the FCPA articulates both ethical and business arguments in support of the FCPA. The House Report declares that the payment of bribes to foreign officials runs "counter to the moral expectations and values of the American public." With respect to economic considerations, the House Report further claims that obtaining contracts through bribery "short-circuits the marketplace by directing business to those companies too inefficient

---

[99] Ibidem.

to compete in terms of price, quality or service." The House concluded that bribery "rewards corruption instead of efficiency."

The timing of the enactment of the FCPA, as discussed in chapter 2, provides a further explanation. To recall, in 1977, the 95th Congress legislated in a substantially less globalized marketplace than does today's 111th. Although on the brink of a decade of economic expansion, Japan had yet to emerge as a major player in international trade and U.S. relations with China were in their infancy. Hence the House Report's references that corrupt payments by U.S. companies "have been made not to 'outcompete' foreign competitors, but rather to gain an edge over other U.S. manufacturers." Congress thus worried that paying bribes abroad would give certain "corrupt" American companies an edge on their more efficient and more ethical American competitors. Foreign competition was not perceived as a meaningful threat in 1977. We believe this different economic landscape, combined, of course, with foreign policy considerations, and perhaps even the national soul-searching that followed the Watergate Scandal, may explain the 95th Congress's willingness to impose a unilateral burden on the international activities of U.S. regulated firms.

But if we want American MNEs to be more successful abroad, and FDI to increase, especially in the last global frontier markets, particularly Africa, the FCPA must be revisited. I am actually not alone in observing that the current U.S. approach to FCPA enforcement is having adverse consequences that should be addressed. Former Attorney General Michael B. Mukasey back in 2011 testified before Congress, making several suggestions as to how the FCPA could be refined and improved. At the time he proposed:

a. Clarifying the definition of terms used in the law, including "foreign official"
b. Adding an affirmative defense for companies that have rigorous compliance programs in place but who find themselves on the wrong end of a criminal probe
c. Adding a "willfulness" requirement for corporate criminal liability

d. Limiting successor liability for the prior corrupt activities of a business that was acquired

e. Improving the way the DOJ provides guidance and advice to companies that are trying to comply with the law; and

f. Limiting a parent company's liability when it did not know about the improper behavior of a subsidiary.[100]

Changes along the lines suggested by Mr. Mukasey could provide companies more certainty as to whether or not their conduct risked violating the FCPA, and taken as a whole they represent an encouraging effort at making the FCPA relatively fairer.

Another proposal that could bring clarity to FCPA enforcement was made by James R. Doty, former General Counsel of the SEC. Mr. Doty suggested that the SEC create a "Reg. FCPA," similar to Regulation D under the Securities Act of 1933 and other administrative schemes, which "would establish a permissive filing regime; by making the filing, a registrant would benefit from a regulatory presumption of compliance."[101]

Under this system, "Reg. FCPA would set forth items required to be described, represented or disclosed, with appropriate exhibits, constituting the registrant's FCPA Compliance Program" and "[t]he filed FCPA Compliance Program would be subject to Staff review and comment, as with the Annual Report on Form 10-K." The SEC would also issue no-action letters based on a corporation's filings. Mr. Doty posits that this system would be relatively easy to administer, and the SEC could use its experience with other similar regulations to ensure that it functions smoothly. Among the benefits that Doty predicts as a result of implementing a Reg. FCPA are that it would:

---

[100] See Foreign Corrupt Practices Act: Hearing Before the Subcomm. on Crime, Terrorism, and Homeland Sec. of the H. Comm. on the Judiciary (June 14, 2011) (testimony of Michael B. Mukasey, Partner, Debevoise & Plimpton LLP).

[101] James R. Doty, Toward a Reg. FCPA: A Modest Proposal for Change in Administering the Foreign Corrupt Practices Act, 62 Bus. Law. 1233, 1234 (2007).

- Focus on questionable behavior and achieve greater deterrence;
- Complement other initiatives, including the OECD Convention and UNCAC; and
- Make U.S. companies more competitive.[102]

These suggestions may help bring greater clarity and, as a result, fairness, without jeopardizing the goals of the FCPA, but they may become cumbersome and do not address directly the crux of the issue: companies subject to the FCPA compete in the same international arenas as companies that are not, but those subject to the FCPA face substantially different rules and enforcement costs.

In conclusion, I am not suggesting any praise to any easement on bribery. I started this book discussing the consequences of corruption to business and society at large. Corruption has a corrosive influence on business, government and society in general. The identification and eradication of corruption provides societal and economic benefits that merit the expenditure of significant private and government resources. Moreover, it is not my place or intention, nor is the scope of this book, to advocate any specific policy proposal. I believe, however that the competitive landscape of the 21st century global economy warrants the reevaluation of the United States' strategy in fighting foreign corruption. I am also of the opinion that the current anti-bribery regime, which tends to place disproportionate burdens on U.S. regulated companies in international transactions and incentivizes other countries to take a "lighter touch," which is causing lasting harm to the competitiveness of U.S. regulated companies and the U.S. capital markets. Lastly, even putting aside the disproportionate costs borne by U.S. regulated companies; the continued unilateral and zealous enforcement of the FCPA by the United States may not be the most effective means to combat corruption globally. In fact, in some circumstances it may exacerbate the problem of overseas corruption.

[102] Ibidem. at 1248 – 53.

Appendix A - FCPA Pocket Handbook

Foreign Corrupt Practices Act - What and Who? [103]

The Foreign Corrupt Practices Act is a federal law enacted in 1977 by the United States of America, prohibiting payment of bribes to foreign government officials and political figures.

There are two provisions to the Foreign Corrupt Practices Act: the anti-bribery provisions, enforced by the Department of Justice, and the accounting provisions, enforced by the Securities and Exchange Commission.

The following entities are particularly prohibited from making improper payments.

- **Issuers** - Companies that have securities registered in the U.S. or are required to file reports with the Securities and Exchange Commission are considered issuers.
- **Domestic concerns** - Any business entity, with its principal place of business in the U.S. or organized under the laws of the U.S., as well as nationals and residents of the U.S. are considered domestic concerns. Both, issuers and domestic

---

[103] Based on World Compliance FCPA guidelines, which can be found at www.fcpa-worldcompliance.com

concerns may be held liable for any act that promotes a bribe, by using the U.S. mail or any means or instrument of interstate commerce or for an act, which occurs outside of the U.S.

- **Foreign nationals and businesses** - A foreign national or business may be held liable for any act that promotes a corrupt payment within the U.S. Unlike the first two entities, foreign nationals and businesses are not liable for acts committed outside of the U.S.
- **Third Parties and agents** - A third party or agent acting on behalf of an issuer, domestic concern or foreign national or business is liable under the same conditions as the issuer, domestic concern or foreign national or business.

Violations of the FCPA

The following five elements constitute a violation of the anti-bribery provision:

- **Payment** - The FCPA states that payments includes offers, payments and promises to pay, gifts, promises to give or authorization to pay, offer or give anything of value. Anything of value includes tax benefits, information and promises of future employment, scholarships, discounts, entertainment, travel expenses and insurance benefits.
- **Foreign official** - The FCPA prohibits payments made to a foreign official, political party, political party official or a candidate for foreign political office. Payments made to third parties are prohibited if the payer knows that the payment is meant for the foreign official, whether direct or indirectly. Knowledge includes deliberate ignorance or conscious disregard.
- **Business purpose** - In addition to a corrupt intent, a payment must be made with the objective of obtaining, retaining and or directing business.

- **Corrupt intent** - Corrupt intent is defined as any payment made with the purpose of influencing an act or a decision, such as:
  - Inducing an official to act in violation of that official's lawful duty
  - Securing an improper advantage
  - Inducing an official to use their influence to affect any governmental act or decision
- **Business purpose** - In addition to a corrupt intent, a payment must be made with the objective of obtaining, retaining and or directing business.

Exceptions to the Rule

Several types of payments are exempt from FCPA regulations, including:

- Payments for routine government actions
- Payments to expedite or secure the performance of a routine governmental action by a foreign official, political party or party official, which are not prohibited.
- Payments, which are lawful under foreign law. A payment is not prohibited if it is lawful under the laws and regulations of the relevant foreign country.
- Reasonable and bona-fi de expenditures
- A payment, which is reasonable and bona fi de expenditure and directly related to the promotion, demonstration or explanation of products or services or directly related to the execution or performance of a contract, is not prohibited.

FCPA Accounting Provisions

Accounting provisions only apply to issuers who are required to keep records and accounts, which accurately reflect the transactions and dispositions of the issuer's assets. A company may be liable if its records:

- Omit a transaction, such as a bribe, illegal commission or other improper payment.
- Disguise records to conceal improper activity or fail to identify the improper nature of a recorded transaction.

Internal Controls

Issuers are required to maintain a system of internal accounting controls to provide reasonable assurances that transactions are executed in line with management's authorization. All transactions must be recorded in a manner that permits the preparation of financial statements that conform with generally accepted accounting principles (GAAP) and to maintain accountability for assets.

The access to assets is allowed only with management's authorization and the accountability for said assets must be compared with the existing assets at reasonable intervals. When identified, appropriate action must be taken with respect to any differences.

Liability for Acts of Subsidiaries

Issuers can be held liable for the conduct of their foreign subsidiaries, even though the improper conduct occurred outside of the U.S. The scope of liability is based on the issuer's incorporation of the subsidiary's financial statements in its own records and SEC filings.

Obligations of Minority Owners

An issuer who owns fifty percent or less of the voting power of another company is subject to modified accounting provisions. It is the issuer's responsibility to use its influence to have the company develop and maintain a system of internal accounting controls.

National Security Exception

The accounting provisions do not apply if an issuer's liability results from its cooperation with the federal government on a matter concerning national security.

SARBANES-OXLEY

Senior management may be liable if they certify statements, which fail to disclose known violations of the FCPA's accounting provisions.

FCPA Penalties

The SEC is charged with enforcing violations of the accounting provisions while the DOJ is primarily responsible for enforcing the anti-bribery provisions. Both agencies can institute civil actions, but only the DOJ is authorized to file criminal charges.

Penalties for individuals: Anti-bribery provisions

- Civil penalty up to $10,000
- Criminal fine up to $250,000 and or imprisonment up to 5 years
- Under the Alternative Fines Act, the fine may be increased to twice the gross financial gain or loss resulting from the corrupt payment
- The company on whose behalf the person acted cannot pay a criminal fine imposed on an individual directly or indirectly.

Penalties for entities: Anti-bribery provisions

- Civil penalty up to $10,000
- Criminal fi ne up to $2 million
- The Alternative Fines Act may increase the criminal fine to twice the gain or loss resulting from the corrupt payment.

Penalties for individuals: Accounting provisions

- Civil penalty up to $100,000
- Criminal fi ne up to $5 million or twice the gain or loss caused by the violation, and or imprisonment up to 20 years
- The company on whose behalf the person acted cannot pay fines directly or indirectly

Penalties for entities: Accounting provisions

- Civil penalty up to $500,000
- Criminal fi ne up to $25 million or twice the gain or loss caused by the violation

FCPA Other Penalties / Sanctions

Other government penalties that apply are:

- Suspension or debarment from securing contracts with the government
- An indictment can lead to suspension
- The suspension or debarment of a business by one government agency disqualifies it from contracting with any other government agency

Private lawsuits:

- No private rights of action
- Securities class actions or shareholder derivative suits.
- Lawsuits based on antitrust laws and common law

Important Elements of Compliance with FCPA regulations

There are a few elements of compliance with the FCPA regulations that one should become familiar with. The following are a list of them.

Compliance Programs

Companies should incorporate compliance programs, policies and training throughout the entire organization, including:

- Training employees on anti-bribery laws and ask them to certify that they understand and will follow corporate policy. Employees should also be informed on the proper procedure and contact channels for guidance and or to report possible violations;
- Verifying that third party relationships, such as joint venture partners and agents, comply with anti-bribery laws;
- Performing in depth due diligence on joint venture partners, agents and targets of prospective mergers and acquisitions;
- Periodic monitoring of third parties to detect entities with close relationships to Foreign Officials or government entities.

Third Party Risk Monitoring

All corporations subject to FCPA regulations should perform a risk assessment on all business partners, third party agents, and potential merger partners to understand whether any company or individual is affiliated with a foreign government.

The purpose of this risk assessment is the detection of bribes and corruption within the third party network, by determining whether foreign officials or state owned enterprises (SOEs) are hiding within the business network. A good first line of defense is the screening of all third parties against a comprehensive database of foreign officials and their family members, SOEs and their executives and directors, to ensure that funds transferred to these entities are not conflicting with the regulations of the FCPA. These screenings should be performed on a regular basis, such as monthly or quarterly, to be protected from frequent changes in the political arena.

Components of the database of Foreign Officials and State Owned Enterprises:

- Contains over 6,000 State Owned Enterprises;
- Contains up to 900,000 known Politicians and family members;
- Contains over 50 percent primary unique identifiers, such as dates of birth, photographs, passport numbers and national id numbers;
- Contains names in primary language such as Chinese or Arabic to increase the screening accuracy.

Attorney General Opinions

Issuers and domestic concerns can contact the Attorney General for guidance concerning whether certain conduct violates the FCPA's anti-bribery provisions. The request must specify exact facts related to the actual conduct, the DOJ does not provide opinions on hypothetical situations.

After a potential violation is discovered, it is recommended to conduct an internal investigation, preferably by outside counsel in the country where the violation took place. It is important to implement prompt remedial and disciplinary action as deemed necessary.

Appendix B – Mini Case Studies

Easy on the Wallet or Easy on the Earth: A Case About Ethics in Sourcing

This is one of a series of fictional case studies based on real international business ethical dilemmas. It is designed to promote questions and commentary. We welcome your participation.

By Meghan Skarzynski, a senior at Santa Clara University, is a Hackworth Fellow at the Markkula Center for Applied Ethics.

Fashionforward! is an online auction site where those who have more style than money can bid on designer apparel. The site registers members for $30, who is then allowed to bid on exceptional deals. In an effort to stand out from the crowded field of online bargain sites, Fashionforward!, reached out to the local community in search of help marketing their company to college students.

Part of this effort included hiring a student intern, Carly LeBlanc. At that point, Fashionforward!, had no formal marketing strategy for targeting consumers. As someone who grew up in the digital age, LeBlanc knew she had to kick start the company on the

Internet. Her marketing knowledge centered on the benefits of viral technologies, especially Facebook and Twitter.

LeBlanc immediately revamped the Fashionforward! Facebook page to make it more user-friendly--adding quizzes, polls, discussion boards, and photo albums--as well as setting Twitter blasts to go off repeatedly throughout the day. During her three-month internship, LeBlanc quadrupled the Fashionforward! Facebook fan base. Her project helped catapult the company into prominence. In the three months of her internship, Fashionforward! increased the number of items offered on the site threefold.

The CEO noticed LeBlanc's success in social networking and asked her to launch a guerrilla marketing campaign on her own campus to create buzz for Fashionforward! among her peers. The CEO challenged her to register 100 new clients within the week.

A member of a sorority since her freshman year, LeBlanc decided to use her Greek connections. She appeared at four campus sororities that week. Promising a free Fashionforward! T-shirt with the sorority's name for every membership purchased, LeBlanc registered 300 new members in one night.

Reporting to work the next day, LeBlanc was excited to share with the team the quick acceptance Fashionforward! had received on campus. She believed she had developed an easy and effective marketing strategy that could be replicated at schools all over the country. LeBlanc planned to order different T-shirt designs for different sororities, highlighting the Fashionforward! logo in bold lettering.

That's when she faced a difficult ethical decision: She could order the shirts from a low-cost company in China or she could order them from a fair-trade company in San Francisco, which provided safe conditions and higher wages for the workers who made the clothing. The fair trade shirts were $28.65, making the grand total for her project $8,595. In contrast, the Chinese T-shirts were $5.50 each, and the company's Web site promised fast and free delivery for a grand total of $1,100.

LeBlanc remembered from her Venture Capital Finance class that startup companies need to focus on making the most money during the first two years. She also knew that the T-shirts from China would be cheaper so that she could create a more elaborate design with more graphics and color. She realized her school was a "testing campus" for Fashionforward! and that if her marketing module worked, her internship work would spread to other college campuses. She thought of how easy it would be for a factory in China to produce large quantities of shirts to give away for free as a promotion that she could promote on the Facebook page she had worked so hard on. She also wondered if the higher cost of the T-shirts would affect the grade the CEO gave her for the internship.

On the other hand, her International Management class had exposed her to the harsh reality of working conditions in China: low wages, rigorous work schedule, poor safety regulations, and the complete lack of worker's compensation and benefits. When LeBlanc had sailed on the Human Rights and Social Justice Voyage with University of Virginia's Semester at Sea, she saw first-hand a Bulgarian clothing factory's destitute environment. She wasn't sure how the public would react if they knew Passionita had taken advantage of outsourcing cheaper t-shirts rather than supporting a U.S. company during the global recession.

Then LeBlanc weighed her other option of ordering t-shirts from a San Francisco T-shirt company she had already used once when she worked with a community service student organization. While the shirts were more expensive, they were fair-trade, organic, and eco-friendly, all attributes she thought would appeal to students. LeBlanc reasoned students would be more likely to wear a shirt that was fashionable and better quality than one that was made cheaply.

LeBlanc didn't want to disappoint her boss. She knew she was working on a deadline and didn't have time to research the prices of T-shirts at other companies. Even though she could have created a bidding war with local T-shirt companies for the business, she preferred to buy from a company that she could trust. At the same time, the $7,495 she would save if she bought from the Chinese manufacturer was too good not to consider. She knew if she made her boss happy, she'd be promoted and enjoy more independence with her future projects.

Discussion Questions

LeBlanc wants Fashionforward! to increase its popularity and become a topnotch company among college trendsetters. What should she do and why?

1. Should she quit her internship and drop the class?
2. Should she ask for an extension on her assignment?
3. Should she order the T-shirts from a fair trade company?
4. Should she assume the Chinese company doesn't treat its workers fairly?

A Time for Ethical Self-Assessment

This is one of a series of fictional case studies based on real ethical dilemmas facing corporate officials and international business. *It is designed to promote questions and commentary. We welcome your participation.*

Focus: Peter Drucker's literature on business scruples and the Ethics of Prudence is newly timely, and not just because of the holidays.

The Drucker Difference December 23, 2008, 12:30PM EST, Rick Wartzman is the director of the Drucker Institute at Claremont Graduate University.

Siemens (SI), the German engineering giant, agreed this month to pay a record $1.6 billion to U.S. and European authorities to settle charges that it routinely used bribes and kickbacks to secure public works contracts across the globe. Prominent New York attorney Marc Dreier—called by one U.S. prosecutor a "Houdini of impersonation and false documents"—has been accused by the feds of defrauding hedge funds and other investors out of $380 million.

And then, of course, there's financier Bernard L. Madoff, who is said to have confessed to a Ponzi scheme of truly epic proportions: a swindle of $50 billion, an amount roughly equal to the GPD of Luxembourg.

All told, it begs the question that Peter Drucker first raised in a provocative 1981 essay in the journal The Public Interest and that later became the title of a chapter in his book The Ecological Vision : "Can there be "business ethics"?"

Drucker didn't pose this to suggest that business was inherently incapable of demonstrating ethical behavior. Nor was he positing that the workplace should somehow be exempt from moral concerns. Rather, his worry was that to speak of "business ethics" as a distinct concept was to twist it into something that "is not compatible with what ethics always was supposed to be."

What Drucker feared, specifically, was that executives could say they were meeting their social responsibilities as business leaders—protecting jobs and generating wealth—while engaging in practices that were plainly abhorrent. "Ethics for them," Drucker wrote, "is a cost-benefit calculation...and that means that the rulers are exempt from the demands of ethics, if only their behavior can be argued to confer benefits on other people."

It's hard to imagine that a Madoff or a Dreier would even attempt to get away with such tortured logic: an ends-justify-the-means attitude that Drucker labeled "casuistry." But we all know managers who've tried to rationalize an unscrupulous act by claiming that it served some greater good.

The Mirror Test

In his book, Resisting Corporate Corruption, Stephen Arbogast notes that when Enron higher-ups sought an exemption from the company's ethics policy so that they could move forward with certain dubious financial dealings, the arrangement was made to "seem a sacrifice for the benefit of Enron." Reinhard Siekaczek, a former Siemens executive, told The New York Times (NYT) that the company's showering of foreign officials with bribes "was about keeping the business unit alive and not jeopardizing thousands of jobs overnight."

For Drucker, the best way for a business—indeed, for any organization—to create an ethical environment is for its people to partake in what he came to call in a 1999 article öthe mirror test." In his 1981 piece, Drucker had a fancier name for this idea: He termed it "The Ethics of Prudence." But either way, it boils down to the same thing: When you look in the mirror in the morning, what kind of person do you want to see?

The Ethics of Prudence, Drucker wrote, "does not spell out what "right" behavior is." It assumes, instead, "that what is wrong behavior is clear enough—and if there is any doubt, it is "questionable" and to be avoided." Drucker added that "by following prudence, everyone regardless of status becomes a leader" and remains so by "avoiding any act which would make one the kind of person one does not want to be, does not respect."

Drucker went on: "If you don't want to see a pimp when you look in the shaving mirror in the morning, don't hire call girls the night before to entertain congressmen, customers, or salesmen. On any other basis, hiring call girls may be condemned as vulgar and tasteless, and may be shunned as something fastidious people do not do. It may be frowned upon as uncouth. It may even be illegal. But only in prudence is it ethically relevant. This is what Kierkegaard, the sternest moralist of the 19th century, meant when he said that aesthetics is the true ethics."

Time to Reflect

Drucker cautioned that the Ethics of Prudence "can easily degenerate" into hollow appearances and "the hypocrisy of public relations." Yet despite this danger, Drucker believed that "the Ethics of Prudence is surely appropriate to a society of organizations" in which "an extraordinarily large number of people are in positions of high visibility, if only within one organization. They enjoy this visibility not, like the Christian Prince, by virtue of birth, nor by virtue of wealth—that is, not because they are personages. They are functionaries and important only through their responsibility to take right action. But this is exactly what the Ethics of Prudence is all about."

Now is the time of year when many of us find ourselves sitting in church or in synagogue, or, if we're not religious, simply taking stock of who we are and where we want to be as the calendar turns. But what's even more critical is that we continue this sort of honest self-assessment when we return to our jobs in early 2009.

"I have learned more theology as a practicing management consultant than when I taught religion," Drucker once said. This, he explained, is because "management always deals with the nature of

Man and (as all of us with any practical experience have learned), with Good and Evil as well."

So take the mirror test now—and then keep taking it well after the Christmas ornaments have been packed away and the Hanukkah candles have burned down to the nub.

Facilitation or Bribery? -- Cultural and Ethical Disparities

This is one of a series of fictional case studies based on real international business ethical dilemmas. It is designed to promote questions and commentary. We welcome your participation.

Geletex, Inc., is a U.S. telecommunications corporation attempting to expand its operations worldwide. As Geletex begins its operations in other countries, it has discovered cultural, governmental, and ethical standards that differ significantly from country to country and from those in the U.S. Geletex has had a code of ethics for its U.S. operations since 1975. The company's director of compliance, Jed Richardson, provides ongoing training for employees, runs a hotline through which employees can report problems, and is well known and respected throughout the company for his high standards and trustworthiness.

As Geletex's international operations grow, Jed is becoming increasingly uncomfortable with what appear to be double standards for the company's U.S. operations and its operations in other countries. Jed, who has been traveling to each of the Geletex international offices, has found the following situations, which since have been causing him sleepless nights:

- In **Lima, Peru**, Jed reviewed financial records and discovered that the commissions expense for the branch was unusually high. Geletex pays its salespeople commissions for each commercial customer they recruit for cellular or long-distance services. Jed knows from experience that some companies pay unusually high sales commissions to disguise the fact the sales personnel are paying kickbacks in exchange for contracts. In the U.S., such payments would be commercial bribery and a clear violation of Geletex's code of ethics. When Jed confronted the Lima district manager and questioned him about the high commissions, he responded, "Look, things are different here. We've got a job to do. If the company wants results, we've got to get things moving any way we can."

- In **Stockholm, Sweden**, Jed noted a number of college age student employees who seemed to have little work to do. Again, Jed questioned the district manager, who responded, "Sure, Magnus is the son of a telecommunications regulator. Caryl is the daughter of a judge who handles regulatory appeals in utilities. Andre is a nephew of the head of the governing party. They're bright kids, and the contacts don't hurt us. In the Scandinavian culture, giving jobs to children is part of doing business."

- In **Mumbai (Bombay), India**, Jed noted that many different payments had been made to both the Indian government and government officials. When Jed voiced his concern, the district manager responded, "I can explain every payment. On this one, we needed the utilities [water and electricity] for our offices turned on. We could have waited our turn and had no services for ninety days, or we could pay to get moved to the top of the list and have our utilities turned on within 48 hours. On the check for licensing, again, we could have waited six months to get licensed or pay to expedite it and be licensed."

Jed is an expert on the Foreign Corrupt Practices Act (FCPA). The act permits "facilitation" or "grease" payments, but prohibits bribes. Facilitation opens doors or expedites processes; it does not purport to influence outcomes. Jed is unsure about Geletex's international operations and compliance with the law. He is very unsure about Geletex having an international code of ethics.

Discussion Questions

1. What ethical standards should Jed develop and apply to Geletex's international operations?

Korean Electronics Maker

This is one of a series of fictional case studies based on real ethical dilemmas facing corporate officials and international business. It is designed to promote questions and commentary. We welcome your participation.

Focus: Blogger Julia Kirby interviews an organizational power expert to gain insight on the corruption scandal at the Korean electronics maker - Harvard Business Review June 21, 2010 3:20 PM EST, by Julia Kirby

---

Samsung's Lee Kun-hee was in power, then out of power, and is now in power again. And that's not making life easy for his former employee Kim Yong-chul. As reported today, the latter is in a form of career exile after accusing his boss and other top executives of corruption. The complaint got results: Lee was removed from the chairmanship of Samsung last year.

But now he's back. Meanwhile, Kim's tell-all book Thinking of Samsung has sold over 150,000 copies but earned him few friends (in public, at least) — and even fewer job offers.

The Christian Science Monitor casts it in the familiar narrative of the "censured and isolated" whistleblower, but it's a far more intriguing tale than that. Kim Yong-chul is no typical organizational eyewitness — he's been a power player in his own right, and tends to give as good as he gets. Earlier in his career, he gained renown as the prosecutor who brought down corrupt South Korean president Gen. Chun Doo-hwan. Even at this low point, Kim retains a kind of power base. Witness his book sales and international press coverage.

When I saw the article, I couldn't resist asking organizational power expert Jeff Pfeffer for his thoughts, since it's the kind of story he loves. Pfeffer has been writing for decades on the political machinations of business people and teaches courses on the subject at Stanford's graduate school of business. (Here's a pdf describing the course "Paths to Power.") His latest piece for HBR is a sort of "how to" guide, offering eleven ways to pull a power play.

Pfeffer saw a number of common themes in the Samsung scenario. In fact, the first thing he did was to caution me not to dismiss it as a curious tale of Korean power dynamics. "The same story plays out, albeit not as dramatically, all the time in U.S. companies," he said. People in positions of authority always shore up their power by dispensing rewards and punishments, coopting antagonists when they can and removing the ones who won't fall into line. People who want more power gain it by pulling surprise moves, by making the most of the resources they control, and sometimes by simply outlasting their rivals.

He wasn't surprised to learn that Kim is spending his days gardening and tending for his pets. Potential employers often shun candidates who are proven troublemakers, even when they are proven right. That's because, whether it's in the context of a Korean chaebol or not, Pfeffer says, "loyalty is valued above all else, including competence." Labor lawyers he knows advise clients not to file suit against their employer, whether for gender or race discrimination or anything else, "unless they plan to earn enough money to not need a job again."

With Lee back in the chairman's seat at Samsung, he's in the kind of role where loyal followers abound and power tends to be self-perpetuating. As Pfeffer sees it, "people and companies with power have the ability to create their own reality. And few are truly interested in siding with, or even getting too close to, people without power."

So is the story over for Kim? He seems to have the power of the western press on his side, and he may even be right. But Pfeffer is afraid that won't be enough: "As the saying goes, if you are going to attack the king, you had better be sure you slay him."

Questions for discussion:

1. So is the story over for Kim? He seems to have the power of the western press on his side, and he may even be right. But Pfeffer is afraid that won't be enough: "As the saying goes, if

you are going to attack the king, you had better be sure you slay him."

Sale of Sand to the Saudis

This is one of a series of fictional case studies based on real international business ethical dilemmas. It is designed to promote questions and commentary. We welcome your participation.

Joe Raymond's position as sales manager for Granite Rock and Sand was in jeopardy. His unit had been low performer in terms of sales for the last seven quarters. Joe's supervisor, VP Tom Haws, told Joe that he had through the next quarter to pull his unit out of last place. Haws also told Joe that Joe would have to be replaced if the improvement did not occur.

Joe and his wife had just purchased their first home. With their mortgage payments totaling $1,200 per month, the loss of Joe's salary would mean the loss of their home.

Following Tom's warning, Joe began interviewing candidates for a vacant sales position in his unit. Joe had conducted three interviews when the final candidate, Jessica Morris, arrived. During the interview with Morris, Joe learned that she was the victim of a layoff by a competitor, Silt, Sand and Such. Joe was not terribly impressed with Morris, but just before she left, she opened her briefcase and offered Joe a sheet of paper bearing the name of an official in the Saudi Arabian government. Morris explained:

When I was with Silt, Sand and Such, we started a program for finding innovative markets for our products. You know, we wanted to tap markets no one had ever thought of. After a lot of research, we discovered that Saudi desalinization plants need a particular type of sand they don't have over there, but we have here. We're the only firm that knows about this. If you hire me, I can see the sale through for Granite.

Morris added: "Look, I need this job. You need your sales up. Think about it and call me."

After Morris left, Joe sat in his office and felt his problems were solved. Or were they?

Discussion Questions

Is Joe's problem resolved? Please explain your answer.

Appendix C - Glossary of Terms

Anti-Corruption – used in reference to a law or act, means designed to eradicate or prevent dishonest or fraudulent conduct.

Anticorruption Law (Brazil) - On August 1, 2013, Brazil enacted a Bill of Law (the "Anticorruption Law") imposing civil and administrative liability on corporations that commit certain corrupt acts. Until now, there was no specific law imposing liability on corporations for corrupt acts committed by their employees or agents. Only individuals could be punished for such violations. Under the new law, both the corporations and the individuals involved in the corrupt activity face liabilities. The law was partly enacted to address the OECD's requirements. In contrast to the FCPA, which requires proof of corrupt intent, the Anticorruption Law is a strict liability statute.

Bribery - is the act of taking or receiving something intended to influence the recipient in some way, in favor of the party providing the bribe. The FCPA makes the bribery of foreign officials illegal.

DOJ - Department of Justice - FCPA matters are handled by the Fraud Section of the Criminal Division of the DOJ. DOJ has criminal FCPA enforcement authority over issuers and their officers, directors, employees, agents, or stockholders acting on the issuer's behalf. DOJ also has both criminal and civil enforcement responsibility for the FCPA's anti-bribery provisions over domestic concerns.

Entity - An entity is a person, partnership, organization, or business that has a legal and separately identifiable existence.

FCPA - The U.S. Foreign Corrupt Practices Act – Enacted in 1977, the FCPA is an anti-bribery act designed to prohibit businesses or individuals from making corrupt payments to foreign officials to obtain or retain business. The FCPA also addresses accounting provisions, enforcing that all businesses keep legitimate records of all finances. The groups included in this act are domestic US businesses, domestic and foreign public companies listed on US stock exchanges, issuers required to file periodic reports with the Securities and Exchange Commission, and foreign businesses acting in the territory of the US.

Foreign official - The FCPA defines a foreign official as any officer or employee of a foreign government, any officer or employee of a foreign department, agency, or instrumentality, and any officer or employee of a public international organization. A "foreign official" could also be someone officially acting on the behalf of these employees/officers.

Instrumentality - In the context of the Act, the broad meaning of "instrumentality" can be understood as government agencies or state-owned and/or state-controlled entities.

Issuer - An issuer is a legal entity, such as a corporation, investment trust, government, or government agency, which is authorized to sell its own securities.

OECD - Organization for Economic Cooperation and Development – Founded in 1961, the OECD is a forum where the governments of 34 democracies with market economies work with each other to promote economic growth, prosperity, and sustainable development. The OECD also works with over 70 non-member countries. The OECD countries can come together to compare policies and internationally comparable statistical, economic and social data through a particular system of peer review.

OECD Anti-Bribery Convention (1997) - The OECD Anti-Bribery Convention establishes legally binding standards to criminalize bribery of foreign public officials in international business transactions and provides for a host of related measures that make this effective. The 34 OECD member countries and six non-member countries - Argentina, Brazil, Bulgaria, Colombia, Russia, and South Africa - have adopted this Convention.

SEC- Securities and Exchange Commission - SEC is responsible for civil enforcement of the FCPA over issuers and their officers, directors, employees, agents, or stockholders acting on the issuer's behalf. SEC's Division of Enforcement has responsibility for investigating and prosecuting FCPA violations. In 2010, SEC's Enforcement Division created a specialized FCPA Unit.

Securities - Securities are financing or investment instruments (sometimes negotiable) bought and sold in financial markets, including bonds, debentures, notes, options, shares (stocks), and warrants.

The Dodd-Frank Wall Street Reform and Consumer Protection Act - "Dodd-Frank" was signed into federal law by US President Barack Obama on July 21, 2010. Passed as a response to the global recession of 2009, Dodd-Frank brought the most significant changes to financial regulation in the United States since the regulatory reform that followed the Great Depression. The Dodd-Frank Act creates the Financial Stability Oversight Council ("Council") to oversee financial institutions.

UK Bribery Act 2010 – Similar to the FCPA, this Act was designed to modernize the bribery laws in the United Kingdom.

However, it is only concerned with bribery. It was enacted to better address the requirements of the 1997 OECD anti-bribery Convention. The act is not concerned with fraud, theft, books and record offences, money laundering offences or competition law.

Whistleblower - A whistleblower is someone who provides information regarding a violation of the securities laws to the SEC. The opportunity to become a whistleblower, and expose FCPA fraud, was created under The Dodd-Frank Wall Street Reform and Consumer Protection Act.

About the Author

Marcus Goncalves, Ed.D.

Dr. Marcus Goncalves has more than 25 years of international management consulting experience in the U.S., Latin America, Europe, Middle East and Asia. Dr. Goncalves is the former CTO and earlier on CKO of Virtual Access Networks, which under his leadership, and project management skills, was awarded the *Best Enterprise Product* at Comdex Fall 2001, leading to the acquisition of the company by Symantec. He holds a master's degree in CIS, a BA in Business Administration, and a doctoral in Educational Leadership from Boston University. He has more than 45 books published in the U.S., many available internationally, in Brazil, Japan, China, Taiwan, Germany, Spain and Romania. He's often invited to speak on these subjects worldwide. Marcus is an Associate Professor and the International Business Chair at Nichols College. He also teaches at Boston University and Brandeis University. He is a visiting professor teaching MBA Project Management courses at Saint Joseph University, in Macao, China, where he also advises on graduate researches. He can be contacted via email at marcus.goncalves@nichols.edu or at marcusg@mgcgusa.com.

References

Barstow, David (2012). "Vast Mexican Bribery Case Hushed Up by Wal-Mart After High-Level Struggle". The New York Times. Retrieved April 23, 2015.

BBC World News. (2011) "News Corp shares hit two-year low on hacking arrest". Retrieved 18 July 2015.

Brooks, Robin; Stacey, Oliver; Jarman, Daniel (2010) "Tackling Corruption and Regulatory Risk in M&A Transactions". Transaction Advisors. ISSN 2329-9134.

Brown, Howard. "$88 Million Fine Agreed by Marubeni Corporation of Japan with the U.S. Department of Justice to Settle a Foreign Corrupt Practices Act Investigation".

Crawford, David; Searcey, Dionne (2010). "U.S. Joins H-P Bribery Investigation". The Wall Street Journal.

Criminal Division of the U.S. Department of Justice and the Enforcement Division of the U.S. Securities and Exchange Commission (2012). "A Resource Guide to the U.S. Foreign Corrupt Practices Act" (PDF). p. 130. Retrieved 23 October 2015.

Fisher, Alice; Greenburg, Douglas; Sabin, Barry; Seltzer, Nathan; Su, Jonathan; Volkman, Eric; Chandler, Kari; Brown Jones, Erin. "DOJ Guidance Underscores Importance of Anti-corruption Due Diligence in International M&A". Transaction Advisors. ISSN 2329-9134.

Funk, T. Markus (September 10, 2010). "Getting What They Pay For: The Far-Reaching Impact Of the Dodd-Frank Act's 'Whistleblower Bounty' Incentives on FCPA Enforcement" (PDF). White Collar Crime Report (Bureau of National Affairs) 5 (19): 1–3.

Graham, Bradley, Stroup, Caleb (2016). "Does Anti-bribery Enforcement Deter Foreign Investment?" (PDF). Applied Economics Letters. doi:10.1080/13504851.2015.1049333.

Hamburger, Tom; Dennis, Brady; Yang, Jia Lynn (April 24, 2012). "Wal-Mart took part in lobbying campaign to amend anti-bribery law". The Washington Post. Retrieved November 18, 2015.

Horn, George (2015). "M and A Due Diligence Failures: FCPA and Goodyear". The National Law Review (Barnes & Thornburg LLP). Retrieved 2 November 2015.

House Committee on Interstate and Foreign Commerce (September 28, 1977). "H.R. Rep. 95-640 REPORT together with MINORITY VIEWS To accompany H.R.3815" (PDF). Retrieved 22 February 2015.

Lawler, William; Phillips, Anthony. "Avoiding the Threat of FCPA Successor Liability". Transaction Advisors. ISSN 2329-9134.

LeRoy Miller, Roger (2011). Business Law Today: The Essentials. United States: South-Western Cengage Learning. p. 127. ISBN 1-133-19135-5.

Luthans, Fred; Doh, Jonathan (2014). International Management Culture, Strategy, and Behavior (9th ed.). New York, NY: McGraw-Hill Education. ISBN 978-0-07-786244-2.

Mandelker, Sigal P.; Emert, Rochelle H.; Caraballo-Garrison, Phillip J. (27 February 2015). "Goodyear Pays for Sins of Subsidiaries in $16 Million Settlement". Proskauer Rose LLP. Retrieved 2 August 2015.

Michael V. Seitzinger (2012). "Foreign Corrupt Practices Act, Congressional Interest and Executive Enforcement" (PDF). CRS Report to U.S. Congress. Congressional Research Service. p. 11. Retrieved 22 August 2015.

Michael V. Seitzinger (2014). "Eleventh Circuit Provides Guidance for the Definition of "Foreign Official" under the FCPA" (PDF). Legal Sidebar via Congressional Research Service. Federation of American Scientists. Retrieved 23 August 2015.

Miguel Bustillo (2012). "Wal-Mart Faces Risk in Mexican Bribe Probe". The Wall Street Journal.

Pelletier, Paul; Tidman, Aaron; Haviland, Jane (2015). "Goodyear's Settlement with the SEC Emphasizes the Importance of FCPA Due Diligence in M&A Transactions and of Having a Robust Anti-Corruption Policy". Mintz, Levin, Cohn, Ferris, Glovsky and Popeo, P.C. Retrieved 2 August 2015.

Posadas, Alejandro. "Combating Corruption Under International Law", School of Law, Duke University.

Reuters (2012). "U.S. says BizJet settles foreign bribery charges". Reuters.

Rich, Ben R. and Janos, Leo (1994) Skunk Works: A Personal Memoir of My Years at Lockheed. New York: Little Brown & Co., , ISBN 0-7515-1503-5.

Richard L. Cassin (2012). "Biomet Pays $22.8 Million To Settle Bribe Charges". The FCPA Blog.

SEC (2010) "SEC Names New Specialized Unit Chiefs and Head of New Office of Market Intelligence" (Press release), Retrieved 23 October 2015.

SEC (2015) "SEC Enforcement Actions: FCPA Cases". 26 January 2015. Retrieved 23 October 2015.

Smith & Nephew (2012). "Smith & Nephew reaches settlement with US Government". Smith & Nephew.

Sprinzen, Nicole; Hildebrand, Jennifer. "DOJ Clarifies Successor Liability for Foreign Acquisitions". Transaction Advisors. ISSN 2329-9134.

Stout, David (2009). "Ex-Rep. Jefferson Convicted in Bribery Scheme". The New York Times. p. A14.

T. Markus Funk, "Another Landmark Year: 2010 FCPA Enforcement Year-in-Review and Trends for 2011," Bloomberg Law Reports (January 3, 2010).

The Washington Post (2012) "Mexican watchdog group says Mexico's federal government should probe alleged Wal-Mart bribes". Associated Press. April 22, 2012. Retrieved November 23, 2015.

US Department of Justice (17 January 2012). "Marubeni Corporation Resolves Foreign Corrupt Practices Act Investigation and Agrees to Pay a $54.6 Million Criminal Penalty".

Welch, David; Weidlich, Thom (April 23, 2012). "Wal-Mart Bribery Probe May Exposes Retailer to U.S. Fines". Bloomberg. Retrieved April 23, 2012.

www.ingramcontent.com/pod-product-compliance
Lightning Source LLC
Chambersburg PA
CBHW061333220326
41599CB00026B/5169